THE FIRE STARTER

THE FIRE STARTER

IGNITING INNOVATION
WITH EMPATHY

APRIL BELL

NEW DEGREE PRESS

THE FIRE STARTER
Igniting Innovation with Empathy

ISBN   978-1-63730-653-6   *Paperback*
          978-1-63730-736-6   *Kindle Ebook*
          978-1-63730-927-8   *Ebook*

To my sweet Autumn.

*My inspiration, my love, my surrender, my return
to grace. I hope the words in this book fall upon
you gently, like golden leaves in the fall, because
by you, they have been brought forth for you.*

CONTENTS

"Mom, just face your fears and when the waves come, they won't knock you down."

— MY DAUGHTER, AGE SEVEN

INTRODUCTION

It was a hot July day—I'll never forget the sizzling heat on our small, red-brick patio. No shade. No trees in our yard. Just the black charcoal pit grill mom used to make dinner many evenings. Our dog was barking—he usually only barked at the cows when they were too close. Or when a car drove up next to the John Deere tractor my dad parked on the dusty road to the side of the house. My brother, sister, and I waited hungrily for dinner, like a pack of dogs. I was seven, my sister five, my brother two. We played aimlessly in the heat while mom whirled about, doing the job of an army to cook dinner, not only for us but for Dad and the rest of the "crew" who were out in the cotton fields. It was half past five. I only know that because that's when we got hungry for dinner. She was frustrated because she could not get the grill started for the burgers. Her burgers were amazing, like everything she cooked. She was the best cook—still is. Her cooking, baking, grilling, or anything that involved creating food was and is truly delicious. But her skill could only be utilized if she could get the fire started.

She yelled out at me: "Make sure your brother stays out of the garden and keep your hands clean." And to my sister: "Stop eating the grass." And to the dog: "Stop your barking—I'll feed you later." And to Dad who was not present: "I hope you're happy with these burgers." And to herself: "If I could just get this thing lit." I stopped to watch her. I wanted Mom to be happy and wondered how I could help. I felt guilty at my lack of success with her first two instructions—we were all dirty and my brother would not stop destroying the still-budding tomatoes.

As I watched her, the next few moments burned into my memory forever, laying down a track which created an immense appreciation for fire... and fire starters. She had disappeared around the corner and reemerged with a gasoline can. And then, in sheer determination as if to will the fire into being, she poured just a bit of gas onto the small flame trying to come alive.

At that exact moment, a West Texas "dust devil," akin to a mini tornado, swirled through our small backyard. The upward gust of wind took the tiny flicker buried deep under the charcoals along with the fresh gas and burst it into massive flames. It was the most incredible sight—like something from a sci-fi movie. I watched Mom throw the gas can urgently to the left behind her. Then I watched transfixed, unable to move, wide-eyed as the flames followed it. As if it were attached by an invisible string. The gas can landed on my two-year-old brother. I remember that flaming gas can flying slowly across the air. I heard screams. It was all so fast... and yet so slow.

The two separate entities became one: the flames and my brother. And then... I saw nothing. I blacked out. Later, after waking up from a black hazy fog, I heard sirens. And my next memory was walking into my brother's hospital room. He was dressed like a mummy. For a seven-year-old who was trying to connect the dots, it was simultaneously humorous and horrifying.

I have had an appreciation for fire starters ever since. I learned well that not everything that can start a fire should be used to start one. And that it takes time to heal from a wildfire.

Just like creating a fire, the right elements must be put in place at the right time. Whether the fire's purpose is for cooking great burgers or keeping a family warm on a frigid day, building a fire is a process, and it requires three key elements:

1. Oxygen—to sustain combustion
2. Fuel—the material that gets burned
3. Heat—to raise material to ignition temperature

When put together, it creates the chemical reaction or "spark" of fire.

Innovation also requires a process and three key elements:

1. Value to me—the leader
2. Value to us—the team
3. Value to them—the user

When put together, it creates the "spark" to ignite innovation. And the secret to getting the right level of spark is empathy.

WHY EMPATHY FOR INNOVATION?

Empathy is "the ability to sense other people's emotions, coupled with the ability to imagine what someone else might be thinking or feeling," according to Greater Good Science at Berkley.

When we innovate, we must create engagement.

To create engagement, we must understand the emotional value.

To find emotional value, we must use empathy.

When we innovate without understanding the emotional value, we reduce the probability of creating or sustaining what we want to innovate. Just like a fire without the proper elements, innovation will not light up or burn for its productive purpose sans empathy.

If we apply too much emotional value on any one of these three elements (Me, Us, or User), we can create an eruptive wildfire, which takes time to heal or repair.

When empathy is applied to innovation in the right time across the three elements of me, we, and user, it creates a valuable innovation equation. Empathy brings us back to what matters most when we are walking through the unknown.

WHY SHOULD YOU CARE ABOUT INNOVATION?

In today's environment everyone is innovating in the unknown.

In a recent survey of senior executives, more than 70 percent said that innovation will be at least one of the top three drivers of growth for their companies in the next three to five years.

Yet, that same study showed that while they know innovation is paramount, 65 percent surveyed were only "somewhat," "a little," or "not at all" confident about the decisions they make in this area.

The reason for the gap is because innovation in most systematized organizations is only a small part of the corporate structure rather than embedded as a key component of corporate culture.

According to McKinsey, "Prioritizing innovation is the key to unlocking postcrisis growth. The COVID-19 pandemic upended nearly every aspect of life, from the personal (how people live and work) to the professional (how companies interact with their customers, how customers choose and purchase products and services, how supply chains deliver them)" (Bar Am, Fursthenthal, Jorge and Roth, 2020).

My goal is to inspire you to see empathy as a powerful way to solve big problems. Our problem-solving skills must become innovative in nature, if we are to create the changes our current environment is requiring us to do.

For any great change to occur, we must use an approach that is proven to bring something new to life. Our empathic approach to innovation is rooted in Design Thinking which was developed at Stanford's d.school and used by IDEO, both founded by David Kelley.

But the exploration in this book goes beyond this process and posits that empathy is more than just the first step of innovation, and empathy is required for more than just the end user. Most importantly, empathy is required for ourselves and for each other as we innovate.

WHY ME?

My work as an empathy researcher and consultant to Fortune 500 companies for nearly two decades has given me a title many of my clients lovingly call "The Empathy Queen." I have been provided many opportunities to see amazing innovation that has reached the masses. Through the lens of empathy, I have helped organizations test ideas, advertisements, and products at every stage of the innovation process.

We do this by uncovering the emotional value to individuals, internal teams, and external end users or customers.

But there's more to the story than my professional experiences. By using the same empathic process and tools on myself as I do for my clients, I have discovered I can recreate my own life. It was through and on the other side of a painful divorce that I noticed this connection.

I started seeing patterns in my therapist's chair that mirrored the chair I had been sitting in as a consultant—these empathic patterns helped me unlock and reframe emotions which lead to inspired and empowered action. The tools I learned about in therapy—how the brain works, attachment theory, the neuroscience behind internal and interpersonal connection—were similar to the tools we used in our empathy innovation sessions.

Slowly but surely, I began to move from a place of fear and anxiety—defense mechanisms—to a place where I used empathy on myself to migrate out of disillusionment. The result was more focused action toward my goals, more sustainable motivation. I began living on purpose—empowered and productive.

In my typical researcher mode, I began to study everything I could get my hands on. From cognitive behavioral therapy, Eye Movement Desensitization and Reprocessing (EMDR), Internal Family System (IFS), trauma informed equine therapy, and neuroscience hacks, I wanted to learn everything I could about the connection between empathy to creative problem solving using the way our brain is wired.

During this process I discovered the most amazing thing: I didn't need to change myself. I only needed to show up a little differently to my own life, with more empathy toward myself and others... the same way I showed up for my clients on every project. What I know now is that my desire to discover others was a hidden deeper desire to discover myself.

It is my intention and purpose in this book to help corporate leaders innovate internally in their organization (we) and, most importantly, within themselves (me) to lead a life transformed from the inside out in the same way they innovate externally for their customers (users).

HOW IS THE BOOK ORGANIZED?

The book is divided into three parts: (1) The Map to Innovating with Empathy; (2) The Barriers to Innovation; (3) The Amplifiers of Empathy.

The chapters in the first part will walk you through the five-step empathy process we use for corporate product innovation (for users) but in a non-traditional format. I will show you the process can be used just as effectively for leader (me) and team (we) innovation as it can be for product innovation. Through stories and examples, we will walk through the five-steps (Desire, Discover, Discern, Design, and Decide) to solve any innovation challenge.

In the second part of the book, "The Barriers to Innovation," I will show you how and why emotions can keep individuals and teams stuck when innovating. By its nature, innovation is disruptive. It can be chaotic. Chaos creates emotions that when kept below the surface are a barrier because they disempower us if they stay stuck. So, we will pull back the mask of emotions that are often not talked about openly—from resistance, perfectionism, confusion, loneliness, rigidity, to overwhelm. And for each, I will show you how empathy can help reframe and use these as gifts for a source of empowerment.

Our third and final part of the book, "The Amplifiers of Empathy" is about how to build your empathy muscle. Often, I get a lot of questions about "how to" be more empathetic. So, we will focus on four key qualities that can help you practice empathy, in any situation. Over time, as you get the hang of these key ingredients to empathy—curiosity, play, detachment, and presence—you will see more than your innovations come to life, you will see yourself living in a more deeply connected and creative way.

WHO IS THIS FOR?
This is for the change makers, the leaders, the exhausted, weary warriors who see the problems and want to be a part of the solution. It's for the seekers.

I wrote this to share what has helped me professionally bring innovation to life, and personally help me innovate my own life. I wrote it for my clients who are brilliant, insightful, and helping others with their empathic leadership. I wrote it for executive leaders who are trying to manage an organization and need new tools to operate effectively across generational and other differences. I wrote this so that we can all look under the mask at each other and find our way back to our common humanity.

I wrote it because I am exhausted living in a world where we are all too exhausted to connect at a deeper level. I wrote it so that we see the value of slowing down to listen to learn from each other.

Because when we can truly see ourselves and each other, beyond the lens through which we were taught to view things, we might all individually and collectively change the world for the better with what we create.

For those of you who are like me, those who love to research and dissect data and language to decide if you agree or not, I want to stop you before we start. It is normal for our brains to "assess data" from our perspective. My hope is you will be open to seeing innovation and empathy from a new lens. And that it will help you leverage the value you can provide as an individual and within your organization during a time when disruptive change is a requirement.

My hope is that as you increase your personal and interpersonal value, you will be led to create purposefully for the sustainability of our planet and people, for the protection of our collective humanity, and for the future provision of our kids and theirs in the most humane way possible.

So, if you tend to get caught up in a definition of a word or the way I think about innovation or perhaps the way I named something, I suggest you move past it. I care about you getting the concepts or walking away with one idea or possibility that helps you shift your thinking. The truth about empathy is that it creates room for our hearts to shift our perspective. I hope your heart and mind expand because of reading.

Because the truth is, we will innovate, one way or another. I am going to show you why it's best to do so with empathy for greater peace, empowerment, and purpose.

This is not a passive read. And you do not have to read it in order. If a chapter speaks to you, reflect on the questions, and let it marinate. See what comes up for you.

Innovation is just a series of small steps—ones of rethinking, shifting, pondering what could be, and then experimenting with more steps toward what you desire most. I will show you why doing so with empathy creates efficiency, so let us begin our journey together, shall we?

PART I:

THE MAP TO INNOVATING WITH EMPATHY

In our fast-paced world, we can feel pressure to act fast and make quick decisions even with the most daunting problems to solve.

But the challenge we face when making quick decisions in the unknown without a proper map is that "quick solutions" may be hard to fix and lead to eventual bigger problems to solve.

As with any map, we are looking for guidance, direction, and context so that we have confidence in our decisions. That's what innovating with empathy does. It provides a process that works because it creates safe decision making. While it may seem counterintuitive and require a bit of slowing down at first, it has been proven to innovate products for abundant growth and it can do the same for people and organizations.

1. Desire – uncover heart-led clarity
2. Discover – expand knowledge by listening to learn from the heart
3. Discern – connect dots to see emotional patterns for design inspiration
4. Design – create passion-led possibilities
5. Decide – determine wise direction from holistic understanding.

Notice that "decide" is the last step in the process. There's a reason for that. This next chapter gives a snapshot of one leader's empathic innovation journey so you can see the impact.

CHAPTER 1:

THE INNOVATOR'S JOURNEY

It was a beautiful fall day in North Texas, with a high of seventy-six and clear skies. I was struck by the peace unnoticed by my friend. He was complaining about his ex and her new fiancé. The birds chirped in my peaceful backyard, dogs playfully gnawed on a bone, horses grazed in the pasture. A fire danced in the fire pit. I was in my zone, connected deeply in conversation in a peaceful setting. I saw the inner turmoil on the deep creases lining his normally smooth face. So, I began to "dig" into what was really going on below the surface of his complaints.

I reflected on how we were here. We met one night over dinner and drinks through friends. I immediately saw his power, his strength. He was tall, broad shoulders, and he had just turned fifty-nine.

I was curious, thinking, *what makes a man with this much presence tick?* And that began our friendship; my curiosity of who he was behind his warrior-like stature led us to a game of pool. I discovered that night there was more beneath his mask of power. He was in pain—his wife had left him six years before for one of his best friends.

He was set to retire. Millions in his bank account. But half of that awarded to her during the divorce. He had risen to the top of his global healthcare company in his over twenty-five-year career. He learned the corporate system. He produced wealth by providing for the system he worked for and in turn had provided for his family.

INNOVATING IS INEVITABLE

Imagine that C-Suite Robert had everything he planned to accomplish: three incredible kids. His family was set. His life was set until his wife left him.

It struck me that sometimes we innovate because we want to disrupt what is not working. And sometimes, disruption causes the need for innovation. Either way, he needed to innovate his life.

WE CAN GET STUCK IN THE UNKNOWN

I could tell he had been stuck for the last six years, and asked, *"What would you do exactly the same if you could do it all over again?"*

He looked at me, puzzled. And after a bit, he answered, *"I wouldn't change anything. I did what I had committed to do."*

"Ok, makes sense," I answered. I decided on a multiple-choice approach. *"What do you want to create? What*

do you want to provide? What is important for you to protect?"

I hit the nail on the head because he answered all three questions with simplicity and clarity. *"I want to create a life that is meaningful—to myself and others. I want to provide value they appreciate. I want to protect my health so that I can create longevity."*

SYSTEMIC RULES DON'T APPLY IN THE UNKNOWN

I exhaled and thought, *Okay, he knows what he wants. Then why is he struggling?*

To him, I asked: *"What is the biggest challenge you face?"*

And then he said something so powerful, in a whisper, *"I don't know how to do it. Everything I try puts me back in the same loop. I did everything I knew to do. I followed the rules and did it 'right' according to what I had been taught. There are no rules to follow in this unknown land I'm in. I don't know how to win anymore."*

INNOVATION REQUIRES BOTH HEAD & HEART

Suddenly, in this powerful man's vulnerability, I had an epiphany. Those in control can lose their power in the unknown. When unpredictably hits, the new rules of engagement are unclear. And without clarity, a mix of fear, sadness and quite often, anger, can seep in. If those emotions stay below the surface, they create a sense of "stuck-ness" and "disempowerment," preventing change or transformation.

He was stuck because he was trying to figure out how to innovate his life from his head, not his heart.

INNOVATION IS A HERO'S JOURNEY

Often, when we think of innovation, we see the final product or result, and believe that is the innovation. But innovation is not the final product, it is the process to develop it. Innovating is a hero's journey. Like journeying into the air in a hot air balloon, innovating is a flight filled with risk, hardship, unexpected challenges, powerful presence, and immense learning. Navigating an open sky full of possibilities and many unknowns is only for the bravest of heroes.

To soar to new heights, the hero must know when to stay grounded, when to ignite the fire, and when to empty the sandbags so that they can launch, fly, and land while navigating the changing weather patterns. As Joseph Campbell puts it in his book, *The Hero's Journey*, "The journey of the hero is about the courage to seek the depths; the image of creative rebirth; the eternal cycle of change within us."

This was the case for Robert. He was about to traverse the journey through innovation like a hero.

Fast forward two years after our discussion in my backyard. Robert is re-married to a woman with three kids.

He has two grandbabies he spends time with regularly. He reconnected to his oldest daughter after a rough patch in their relationship. He is on the board of directors of one non-profit, and self-funding a new effort to feed the hungry in five cities across the United States. He helps his wife run her business with his leadership expertise. This is all in addition to serving as a leader in the corporation he "grew up" in.

His life is full, his mind active, along with his heart. It is because he innovated his life using empathy as the cornerstone. Empathy allowed him to walk through the journey to spark the fire and keep it lit.

Here's the Five-Step process he used.

THE HERO'S INNOVATION JOURNEY—EMPATHY CO-CREATION™

1. **Desire—create based on heart-led clarity.**
That night, before we departed, I asked him: *"Can you help me understand more about what you want for your future?"*

He always says yes when I ask this way. I was glad he had said yes.

"You mentioned 'creating a life that is meaningful, providing value, and protecting your health.' Will you find some imagery or pictures that characterizes the experience you envision with each of those?"

He chuckled endearingly toward me and said, *"Yes April. I'll do this for you."*

"Thank you," I said. *"I really appreciate you helping me see what you see."*

A few weeks later, we got together again, and his excitement was evident. It was much different than the deeply-lined wrinkles. He smiled and we embraced. Then he began talking about how a picture of a soccer player scoring a goal gave him a sudden realization. He saw a metaphor about his life being a game. *"I realized my life isn't over. I just missed scoring a goal."* As he showed me each of the images, telling me the story of each and why, I could see how he had moved from confusion to clarity in what he desired.

Because now, he had connected to more than a rational goal—he knew emotionally why it mattered.

2. **Discover—listen to learn from the heart to expand knowledge**
He continued to talk about how his dreams would come to life—how he would approach work differently, do volunteer work to help the hungry, and find a healthy romantic relationship.

But then something shifted. I saw his excitement fade. A sense of anxiety took its place.

I noticed statements transition to questions. And the questions had a pattern—they all began with "how." I gently mirrored questions back to him.

"*Robert,*" I stopped him. "*What is one area where you are passionate but need to learn more?*"

He said, "*Volunteering. But I don't know how it's possible to manage volunteering with everything else I have on my plate.*"

He paused, then continued, "*I have no idea how to find an organization that fits what I am passionate about. When I did the vision exercise you gave me, I realized seeing poverty when I was young is what fueled my own success. I swore I would never deal with poverty.*" He hesitated, drew in his breath, then said, "*And now I want to help those who are in need.*"

"*Great! That's a perfect place to start. May I make a suggestion?*"

Half interested, half annoyed, he responded: "*Okay, go ahead.*"

"*Can you think of three to five people successful in their career and doing something to give back to others?*"

He looked off, pondering. Then said, "*Yes, Don an ER doctor. He serves on a ministry board for doctors who provide medical care in South America. He goes twice a year and always comes back talking about it. Oh, and Rick—he helps boys' basketball teams in inner cities.*"

I stopped him. *"Okay perfect, you can think of more later. Find a time to meet with them—either over coffee or a call. Ask a few questions about their story on how they began their journey helping non-profits."*

"But I don't know what to ask. and I already think I know why they do it. Not sure that would help."

"For now, please leave all beliefs about who they are or how they got involved. Instead, just pretend you don't know anything. Try to understand their 'why'... from their perspective."

I waited for him to respond. Puzzled, he said: *"I'm not sure how this is going to help. It seems like a distraction. Wouldn't it be better to learn about the different organizations I'm most interested in?"*

I responded, *"Trust me. You will learn more of what you need to know in twenty-five minutes of a conversation with these men listening to learn than ten hours of research and analysis on your computer."*

This convinced him that it would be worth his time to do the exercise. But I added, *"This only works if you're willing to stay curious and ask questions to follow your curiosity as you're talking to them."*

3. **Discern—connect dots to see emotional patterns for design inspiration**

We met two weeks later. This time, he brought his computer. *"April, I learned so much. And I have pages of typed* notes. *It was extremely insightful, but after a few days sitting with it, I'm not sure what to do with the information."*

I responded: *"Oh, good, so now you have the emotional data you need."*

He looked confused. *"Say what? Did you just say emotions and data as if they go together?"*

"Yes, I'll show you how to use it—but you're not going to analyze it the way you normally analyze data. You're going to play with it."

He looked at me incredulously with his eyes and said, *"You've got to be kidding—play with it?"*

"Work with me." I maintained my position. And I proceeded to ask him about what he learned. He described how he was able to see something new—for example, he had never considered playing basketball with inner city boys to get involved in an organization as his friend had done.

He also saw a common theme emerge throughout the men—each one believed they would be the one "giving" to the non-profit, but as they became involved, they described *"receiving more than I gave."*

"Great—so I would recommend pulling the data off your computer and instead, use Post-its so you can play with the information a bit more. This will help you further break apart disparate data to see additional themes."

And through the questioning, his recall and notes, along with markers and a dry-erase wall, we created a visual map of his learnings. Soon, the wall was filled with the analysis—and definitive learnings to act on. We parted with him deep in thought. I smiled as we hugged good-bye. I could sense a difference in him, and it was amazing to see.

4. Design—ideate and create passion-led possibilities
This time I didn't have to wait for an in-person meeting. He was stuck. I accepted his invitation to a Zoom meeting, curious where he was stuck. I assumed it was migrating what he had learned to actual designs or "prototyping" ideas. But I was incorrect—instead, he had several scenarios of his "Future Life" on separate Power Point slides. And they were all very different from each other:

    a. Volunteer one day a week for one non-profit organization
    b. Join an online dating app
    c. Meet with a group of "supporters" every other week for coffee
    d. Call each of my children once a week

After reading, I said, *"This is great. As you think about these, what comes up for you?"*

He responded, *"Excited and terrified."*

I chuckled because I'd never heard him use two emotions in one sentence. *"Yes, this is so common. Part of designing is to generate as many ideas as possible. It can be both rewarding and overwhelming. So, let's break it down and chew it, one bite at a time."*

As he broke down his designs further and "tested" the ideas against his own line of questioning, he was able to create a quick hit list for small next steps:

- Have my assistant find contact information for each organization
- Ask two people who were successful with online dating about the apps
- Set two mornings in my schedule when I can break free
- Ask each of my children what time works best for a weekly call

5. **Decide—determine wise direction from holistic understanding**
I noticed more time than normal had lapsed since our last meeting. I was curious if he was stuck. It turns out he was the opposite of stuck. He was moving forward purposefully with great momentum. When I finally heard from him, he seemed different. Clear. Grounded. In control. Confidence exuded from him.

"April", he said reflectively. *"This process has changed my life. I am passionate again and grateful. But my life is so full that something has to give. And I don't know what to let go of. I am not stuck, but I am a little overwhelmed."*

"Ah, yes, you are ready to discern—let's see what you know to decide with wisdom. You have all the answers at this point."

I led him through some questioning to help him reduce the clutter. He was on the verge of creating a life he wanted to live. He just needed some refinement.

Decisions are easier when we have guardrails – they make decision-making easier to see what does and does not work.

Guardrails allow us to not walk off the same cliff each time. They are the criteria for which we move our ideas into reality. Eventually, Robert began to see the patterns he had created with women. He created a set of guardrails and weighed each possible woman against them:

• Does she display confidence?
• Is she authentic?
• Does she have a passion for things in her life?

He also developed guardrails for the non-profit he would be a part of:

• Did they function with a history of success?
• Were they frugal in their administration?
• Could they show evidence of the impact they made?

EMPATHY PROVIDES A PEACEFUL PATH THROUGH THE INNOVATION JOURNEY

Robert created a life he desired by using the power of empathy to navigate the unknown. Through internal and external inquiry into the heart of the matter, he not only used the pain of his previous marriage to help a non-profit in need, but he also connected more deeply with a trusted circle of advisors. And he met and married a woman who shared his passion for helping the underprivileged. She was mentoring one of the inner-city kids' moms!

While this is one individual's journey of using the power of empathy to ignite innovation into his life, it is something anyone can do regardless of what is being innovated.

Like Robert's experience, the emotional challenges are often the biggest enemies of innovation. They are less predictable. Emotions are easy to mask. But empathy allows emotions to surface so they can enlighten and empower purposeful momentum for any innovation.

FIRESTARTER SPARKS – EMPATHY HELPS THE INNOVATOR BECOME THE HERO

1. Innovating is Inevitable
2. We Can Get Stuck in the Unknown
3. Systemic Rules Do Not Apply in the Unknown
4. Innovation Requires both Head and Heart
5. Innovation is a Hero's Journey
6. The Hero's Innovation Journey—Empathy Co-Creation™
   a. **Desire**—create based on heart-led clarity
   b. **Discover**—listen to learn from the heart to expand knowledge
   c. **Discern**—connect dots to see emotional patterns for design inspiration
   d. **Design**—ideate and create passion-led possibilities
   e. **Decide**—determine wise direction from holistic understanding

7. Empathy Provides a Peaceful Path through the Innovation Journey

FIRESTARTER FUEL—IGNITING ME
1. What changes in your life feel out of your control?
2. What "step" in the innovation journey would help you feel more empowered?
3. What choice do you have now that is totally in your power?
4. What small step forward would give you a sense of momentum?

FIRESTARTER FUEL—IGNITING WE
1. What "step" in the innovation journey is your team on right now? What is keeping the team there?
2. What is the biggest challenge your team faces with innovating?
3. If everything else remained the same and you could only change one thing on your team, what would it be? What could you do to impact that?
4. If you had it your way, what would the team do to create momentum?

CHAPTER 2:

DESIRE

Two years into our marriage, my husband and I decided it was time to create a baby. I was thirty-seven with a history preventing me from getting pregnant easily.

We did everything we were told to do. We followed the plan, visited doctors, injected fertility drugs. When that did not work, we tried harder with more extreme hormones. My body much like a heifer on my parent's ranch methodically prepared for the purpose of pro-creation. We were all in on this desire.

It was a lot of work and not pretty. Many nights were full of despair, disconnection, and worry. I was passionate although, like most creations, much was out of my control.

And suddenly, after eighteen months of dedication, we were pregnant! "We did it! We're having a baby! We told everyone we knew. The trying times were behind us... or so it seemed.

INITIAL DESIRE CAN GET LOST IN THE INNOVATION JOURNEY

I was not prepared at our two-month ultrasound for the nurse's expression. I knew before she said it. Her expression told me what she did not have to: "I'm sorry. We can't find a heartbeat."

"What?" I screamed inside. To her, steadily, "What do you mean, you can't find a heartbeat?" I looked over at my husband, hoping he could help me comprehend this statement. Everyone's eyes turned down.

The baby was gone. "You have plenty left to try with," she said cheerily, speaking of the nine other frozen embryos waiting to be thawed, but I refused to listen to her any longer. In that moment, I shut down. I lost desire for what I was trying to create.

WE CAN GET STUCK WHEN EMOTION IS SUPPRESSED

I needed to retreat to a place no one could find me—a storm cellar. I went down, locked the door, and threw away the key to desire. I had given my best effort and lost the battle. As I stayed in my storm shelter, I could not hear the voices above calling down to me, hands outreached, wanting to pull me out. I didn't want to go back to the land of the living up the stairs. A part of me had died with this tiny seed.

I stayed in a state of fear and loneliness for a while. Eventually, my sadness turned to bitterness. And I got stuck.

The problem isn't the emotion we have. The problem is getting stuck in the emotion. When we are unable to access our feelings and question reflectively, we cannot move through the emotion. So, we stay questioning from a place of disempowerment, without answers. Absent of answers, we cannot build a creative solution.

HARNESSING EMOTION TRIGGERS DESIRE

Channeling emotion is needed to get out of the storm cellar and imagine again. Imagination creates vision and vision is activated through empathy. In my case, the trigger came in an unusual form. It changed everything for me—it helped me harness emotion. A friend, let's call her Malinda, called one day. Still in a funk, depressed at my situation, I grimaced when I heard her cheery voice on the other end of the line.

"Guess what—I have some greaaaat news to share!" she said.

I felt even more nauseous than I had before answering. Swallowing the emotion of jealousy toward her chirpy attitude, I asked in an equally bright tone: *"What's up?"*

She replied: *"We're pregnant! Can you believe it?"*

First, my spirits tanked. Then something inside me snapped. I stopped listening. Then, my numb apathy shifted. Suddenly, a fire of desire lit up inside me—anger ignited it.

This was a woman who consciously announced openly she "never wanted to be pregnant because I do not want it to ruin my body." Instead, "maybe I will adopt some day" she told me regularly knowing my deepest desire was to be pregnant.

The rolling emotions were swirling below the surface of apathy—grief, bitterness, sorrow, and loneliness, giving way to loathing anger. First at her, then God, the medical team, everyone. "How dare she tell her news without sensitivity to what I had just been through?" I thought to myself.

ANGER CAN FUEL DESIRE

I learned earlier in life to curb my anger. Acting on it "never turns out well, April." I had heard it 1000 times. Instead, it simmered beneath the surface. So, I seethed in my anger for a few days... and then used it to my advantage.

Karla McLaren talks about the gifts of every emotion in her book *The Art of Empathy*. She mentions anger is one of the most useful emotions because it provides data to explore internal questions.

I didn't know it at the time, but I used anger as a gift—for information and energy. My questions were:

1. What is working in my current situation?
2. What is not working in my current situation?
3. What do I desire most?
4. What choice can I make based on what I desire?

EMPATHIC QUESTIONING RETURNS US TO DESIRE

That's exactly how I used anger—to question with empathy, objectively to understand what was happening below the surface. My anger, as I allowed empathy in, releasing what was not working and embracing my desire, turned into passion. I realized that my dream for a baby did not die with the one I lost. And I knew I needed to try again. I needed to transfer one of the waiting embryos into my body.

There's nothing like a deadline to get us moving back into our dreams. With this fresh perspective and passion fueling me, a deadline presented itself. My husband had decided to leave a company who, to our blessing, was paying for fertility medicine. If I wanted to make another attempt, the time to do it was now.

The operation was scheduled within the week. But that too, created disappointment.

YOUR DESIRE IS MORE IMPORTANT THAN OTHER'S OPINIONS

As they rolled me into the waiting room after making the transfer, the endocrinologist, said: "The embryo has less than one percent chance of becoming a viable fetus. Further, all your other embryos were poor quality. This was the best and it's only a Grade C. The rest were thrown out."

He was better with science than with bedside manner.

He went on: "Don't get your hopes up—you'll likely be in my office starting again soon." He patted me on the shoulder and walked away. I noticed his comment start to deflate my desire and sadness set in. Until I remembered why I was here. I was here because my desire was to get pregnant.

DESIRE IS MAINTAINED WITH RESILIENCE AND HOPE

My anger popped up her head, *"Seriously? Who tells someone that when they are horizontal and helpless? Someone who sees me as a cow, not a human, that's who."* And as I recognized and released my anger, with hands clenched laying there on the gurney, I made a choice, "No," I said, "he does not get to kill my desire. I choose to retain hope."

On day five I took a pregnancy test, trying to sustain hope without it escalating. It was positive. I held my breath for another five days. When the blood results came back, the light inside me turned on. "Not only are you very pregnant, but the heartbeat is strong enough to be twins!" the nurse said with a smile.

I smiled too. My husband looked concerned at the idea of twins. That is the day I knew our creative endeavor would come to life. The day the journey of our greatest creation began. The day faith was restored. I could see that resilience and hope helped bring our desire to life.

Up until this incident, I was ashamed of my anger. But there are moments in life when the beliefs we have come tumbling down. That day, anger became a gift. It helped create the biggest gift of my life—my daughter.

INNOVATION MUST START WITH DESIRE FOR GREATER RESILIENCE

When trying to make big change or innovate, we jump into the complexity required without capacity for the mental effort or energy needed. This can quickly lead to exhaustion, stress, and eventual burnout. But when innovation begins with heart-led desire, it creates vision. Vision drives a project forward if the vision is kept in sight.

It drives action from the longings of the heart. To create something new, it must be activated with a deeper longing or a why behind the goal you're committed to.

DESIRE AWAKENS PASSION AND HOPE

The reason starting innovation with desire is so important is because it helps create resilience throughout the creative unknown. It awakens our passion.

In a study published in Social Neuroscience, researchers collected date on undergraduates at Case Western University. Students were given two "styles" of interviews:

• future based with "positive" open-ended questioning
• past performance based with "assessment" questioning

As predicted, both MRI measurements on brain activity and a follow up interview indicated students who received the first style of future based questioning were inspired and experienced hope. They showed a greater level of:

1. Visual processing and perceptual imagery regions of the brain
2. Global processing—big picture thinking linked to positive emotions
3. Empathy and emotional safety—revealing what they desired helped students feel secure to open up socially
4. Motivation to proactively pursue lofty goals—rather than act defensively to avoid harm or loss

Creating individual desire is even more powerful when working in teams, even though it often doesn't seem that way in many organizational settings.

We see the impact in sports when teams are coached individually and as a team. Teams who have a culture of creating space to dream about "what could be" inspire and make massive impact. That's why movies like Hoosiers and Rudy or the TV series Ted Lasso connect so emotionally—they inspire the rest of us to do the same. Big impact can be made in organizations by establishing vision in the same way vision impacts winning in sports.

TEAMS WHO VISION TOGETHER CREATE BETTER TOGETHER

I remember well the day I received a call from one of my clients about a project. He understood the power of creating desire with his team.

"April, we need you for a nine-day project. When are you available?" said my client on the other end of the phone.

Me to myself: *Ummm, never.* And then out loud, "Well, I need to look at my calendar. Can you tell me more about what you're envisioning?"

The voice on the line: "We're going on a nine-day bus tour discovery excursion. I am hand picking a small team, and I need you to conduct interviews and co-lead the ideation sessions with another agency. Don't worry, it will be worth your time."

When I hesitated, "Imagine for a second helping us overhaul an important piece of business. We need to renovate a processing plant. What we learn on our road tour will give us much needed direction." He worked for a Fortune 50 global food manufacturing company and as he talked, my curiosity grew.

"So anyway, get ready, you're on the rock star crew!" And with that, he hung up. The deal done. I guess I was going on a bus tour. "Okay. This should be interesting."

It was 2005, not long after Hurricane Katrina when the seven of us climbed the steps of what I lovingly called our "rock star" bus. We were united on a quest.

BEGINNING INNOVATION WITH DESIRE GROUNDS A TEAM IN THE "WHY"

Once seated on the bus, I looked around. We looked more like a crew straight out of Ghostbusters than the cool rock-star band I had envisioned. An unlikely cast of characters, but each with our unique strengths. We all believed in his passion.

I wondered if everyone else was as nervous as I was—of what to expect in such a confined space. "Will I add enough value? What is the purpose of us all being here?" I asked myself.

But he was on fire as he described why we were there. He helped us imagine a changed future. "Can you see it?" he said as he looked out into the distance beyond the windows of the bus. I looked behind me trying to see what he was seeing. I realized what he was visioning was only in his mind. And even with my resistance, I could begin to see what he described.

It was not long until he lifted us off the bus in our minds, envisioning a revamped processing plant instead of the one about to be shut down. We could see a future where men and women could keep their jobs. Where a new product could be developed, based on what consumers really wanted.

His vision created images of why we were doing the work. They eased us out of individual anxiety and motivated us to form a unified team. Soon we were buzzing, laughing, beginning to plan the adventure.

TEAMS WHO KNOW THEIR "WHY" CREATE BETTER TOGETHER

We had more than a common purpose—we had a mission. We explored far and wide—our tour route included Dallas, Austin, Houston, Fort Worth, and Saint Louis. We visited restaurants and retailers from Sephora to Academy to Target.

We cried and held hands with Hurricane Katrina victims in Houston, we learned about the families of employees at the processing plant, and tailgaters at a football game at UT in Austin. The more we learned, the more our desire fueled passion to solve the emotional needs in both consumers and employees.

And new ideas were created. The momentum was built, ideas flowed and individually we continued our commitment as a team with a common why.

EVEN CONNECTED TEAMS WITH STRONG VISION HIT A WALL

Until Day 3. We were coming back onto the bus after a day of exploring in restaurants, retailers, and pubs. It was time to share learnings and build on each other's ideas.

You could sense the camaraderie as the team re-entered the bus container. Post-its filled the walls of our bus as we posted feverishly, moving thousands of ideas from heads to paper.

That's when the wheels came off. Figuratively, that is, although I wish they had physically also so the bus would stop moving, and I could jump off.

One of the team members was telling us a story: "You'll never believe this guy – he was eating ribs, downing with beer, and then...." Before he finished, one of the guys from the agency interrupted, "Okay, it's time to start making some decisions. Let's decide on some ideas." At that moment, the energy shifted.

I don't know if it was his abruptness, or adrenaline decreasing, but... it took a turn for the worse. The guy who had been interrupted kept talking, ignoring the command.

Things unraveled further. When you're on a bus rolling seventy miles per hour down the road, it's a little awkward to hit this wall. Difficult to "leave the room." As the tension escalated, the guy from the agency started crying. We all stared around awkwardly, wondering where to put our hands and eyes—these were pre-cellphone days. Thank you, Steve Jobs.

"HITTING THE WALL" SENDS INDIVIDUALS TO INSTINCTIVE SURVIVAL MODE

Just as in Joseph Campbell's The Hero's Journey when the hero "hits the abyss and rebirth occurs." Or in Ed Pixar's book, Creativity, in Act 2, where the protagonist looks for every easy way to solve the problem but cannot solve it without vulnerability and eventually, bravery. And Brené Brown's example of it as "Day 2" when a "breakdown" occurs and everything falls apart in her Unlocking Us podcast. That's what happened to us.

Our team spent a significant amount of brain power taking in and sorting new information and connecting new ideas. From a neuroscience perspective, our brains were fatiguing in this unknown space (afMRI study, 2013). We needed to go back to "statis"—what we knew. With a team whose neural pathways are firing in the amygdala, individual behaviors become reactive toward each other. Thus, we lose our ability to create and relate in the team effectively.

LEADER VULNERABILITY CREATES TEAM DESIRE

What happened next changed everything. Our trusted leader walked the two to three steps to the back of the bus and took a deep breath. We were silent. Then he turned toward us. And with clarity of purpose, in two long steps, he wrote one word on a blank flip chart paper: Success?

Quietly, he said: "I'm curious what success looks like to each of you. But first let me tell you what it means to me. I had this vision I could do something crazy. That we could create powerful change. I convinced leadership to let us learn out of the box. And they believed in me by giving me a big check.

Each of you were selected because of your unique capabilities. I can't do it without any of you. Success to me is that we work to create together the best we can. Because honestly, if we can't, then I fail."

And in turn, we each, with the same vulnerability, explained what success meant to us and why. Slowly, we made our way back to a common desire, and a part of creating something transformative.

He moved us from fear and shame and returned us to hope going from our amygdala to the creativity center of the brain. And he did it through the power of desire.

Desire begins the innovation process because it grounds us in the "why" before we begin. Once we have the awareness of our desire inside us, this awareness brings us home when we lose our way.

FIRESTARTER SPARKS—EMPATHY UNCOVERS DESIRE FROM HEART-LED CLARITY

SPARKS FOR ME

1. Initial Desire Can Get Lost in the Innovation Journey
2. We Can Get Stuck When Emotion is Suppressed
3. Harnessing Emotion Triggers Desire
4. Anger Can Fuel Desire
5. Empathic Questioning Returns us to Desire
6. Your Desire is More Important than Other's Opinions
7. Desire is Maintained with Resilience and Hope
8. Innovation Must Start with Desire for Greater Resilience
9. Desire Awakens Passion & Hope

SPARKS FOR WE

1. Teams That Vision Together Create Better Together
2. Beginning Innovation with Desire Grounds a Team in the "Why"
3. Teams Who Know Their "Why" Create Better Together
4. Even Connected Teams with Strong Vision Hit a Wall
5. "Hitting the Wall" Sends Individuals to Instinctive Survival Mode
6. Desire Returns Teams to Connected Creation
7. Leader Vulnerability Creates Team Desire

FIRE STARTER FUEL

FIRESTARTER—IGNITING ME

1. What is working in your current approach?
2. What is not working?

3. What do you want most from this endeavor and why is it important?
4. What do you still need to learn?
5. What will you gain or who will you be as a result?
6. What do you vision as success?
7. What next step could you take based on what you're seeing?

FIRESTARTER—IGNITING WE
1. What is the team's desire for innovation or transformation?
2. Why is it important for the team to bring this to life?
3. What are the individuals on the team committed to?
4. What do each of the individuals receive from being involved?

CHAPTER 3

DISCOVER

There were only two of us in the room. His eyes were kind, his button-down blue ironed shirt and pleated khakis were business casual. He didn't look at his phone although I could see it buzzing. He wanted to help me understand. We were in the "front room" in a focus group facility in Houston, Texas. My clients were in the "back room," listening intently. They knew him through their business dealings.

A few weeks earlier I received a call from the Vice President of Sales saying, *"I need help understanding something a little... unique."*

I perked up, excited for an opportunity to help a team learn something new. *"Tell me what you're thinking..."*

STRATEGY DOES NOT LEAD TO LEARNING, LEARNING LEADS TO STRATEGY

"I want to better understand a group of energy brokers. We have a love-hate relationship. But I need to learn more, so I know how to win with them. We are doing a lot, but it's mostly based on gut. We keep hitting our head against the wall because nothing is working. Each of our strategies has failed. If we don't do something different, we lose them, and it will be a huge revenue loss for the company.

As I sat listening to my client describe his problem, I could hear many of his beliefs about these brokers rise to the surface. Brokers served the role of an outsourced energy sales team. Every deal made was worth millions plus long-term revenue due to contract length. But the brokers were "not loyal," and they were concerned about being undercut by their competition.

"What do you want to learn?" I asked.

DISCOVERING EMOTIONAL DESIRES & CHALLENGES DISRUPTS FALSE BELIEFS

We sat down and designed and executed a discovery method to learn more about these brokers. "Who were they?" they wanted to know. "What were their struggles, desires, challenges, and goals?"

It was interesting to observe the team as we moved into the interviews. The sales team listened initially disdainfully in the back room as they watched through the one-way mirror. They did not believe what was being shared with me by the brokers I interviewed in the "front room." It was not what they expected to hear.

Every time I went into the back room for their questions, I would hear comments rather than questions. Things like:

"He doesn't believe that," from one team member. And another, saying, "I'm not sure that's really true."

LISTENING TO LEARN IS CONTAGIOUS

But after interview five on Day 2, one team member who had been quiet spoke up, stopping the banter: "Hey, we don't have to believe what they're saying. But our team invested a lot to hear it. So, let's at least listen to see what can be learned. We can decide later what to do with it."

And that's when things got interesting...

One member speaking up, wanting to understand, shifted the rest of the team. As they began listening to learn, they began to see patterns. And once they heard similar sentiments from multiple brokers, they became curious to learn more.

For example, the team came in believing their biggest problem to solve was pricing versus the competitors. But they realized that brokers wanted to be complimented for their efforts. Their deepest desire was to be respected. When they felt respected by larger energy companies, they were more likely to do business with them.

SOLVING PROBLEMS WITH CURRENT PERSPECTIVE DEFEATS THE POINT OF INNOVATION

While this may seem obvious from the outside, it is very common for leaders within companies to get tangled up in the problem. Trying to fix a problem from only one perspective, the current one, defeats the point. Discovery is the way to expand knowledge, and through a different lens, new possibilities arise.

What this company discovered is that by approaching the problem with an empathetic lens, by listening to learn, they could get outside of their judgment. A new perspective gave the team new possibility for creating a win/win relationship with the necessary brokers.

DISCOVERING WITH EMPATHY CREATES EXPONENTIAL POSSIBILITY

After the research, we defined the main themes from our discovery. Then we conducted a day-long ideation session where several strategies were developed to change the broker dynamic. Eventually, they aligned on a new strategy, one based on "building relationships first." And, the broker business was overhauled.

They not only strengthened their relationships, but revenues doubled in year one and tripled by year three. Even more amazing, their model for relationship building externally became the backbone of their internal corporate culture. Because their perspective had changed— from protecting what's "ours" to strengthening what is "ours together."

When you discover, with an open mind, what the truth is for someone else, it connects you to your own truth. This is called perspective-taking.

PERSPECTIVE-TAKING BUILDS A BRIDGE, EMPATHY CROSSES IT

In a recent interview I conducted with Katja Cahoon, a leading Certified EMDR (Eye Movement Desensitization and Reprocessing) therapist and LCSW (Licensed Clinical Social Workers), MBA in California's Bay Area, she explained what happens from a psychological perspective: "When we are stuck in the story, we can't see a way out. Pausing allows us to get into a mind state as an observant thinker rather than chattered thinking. That's because it moves our blood flow from our area of the brain where fight or flight occurs and back into our pre-frontal cortex."

When we move past our own perceptions and begin taking the perspective of others, it has the possibility of building a bridge. But that bridge can only be built if we allow empathy to enter in. That's because "perspective-taking" is a cognitive function.

Empathy takes it a step further allowing you to understand what somebody else feels, according to the UT Research Showcase, McCombs School of Business: "Empathy pulls you out of your head and toward the other person."

Empathic discovery is a state of mindfulness. One where you remove your thoughts from the incessant thinking to wondering. This creates more powerful solutions by tapping into the hearts of others.

When innovating, we can build a bridge between the gap of what we know to be true and what others know to be true using both perspective-taking and empathy.

Combining "my truth" with "another's understanding of truth" allows a more holistic view of truth that goes beyond the mind and into the heart. Then, bigger ideas occur.

Ideas that bring about greater good for the whole are ones where empathic discovery is also used to "test" the common beliefs. Discovery takes us to greater truth based on common human emotional truths. Whereas common culture and beliefs keep us in the weeds. I first learned this in my small high school. I was a junior.

DISCOVERY HELPS US BETTER UNDERSTAND "COMMON TRUTHS"

I remember the rumors about satanic cults well as a teen-ager in the eighties. For a while, it was all we heard or talked about. Talks of buried cows, rings of fire and people buried in the name of Satan hit the nightly news when a "ring of Satanists" was discovered not too far from my town in West Texas.

Not long after, in our small school's hallways, this news became "real."

I walked to my locker, hurrying, late (yet again) for class. That is when I heard it, the girls near the locker whispering. One of the blonde-headed cheerleaders. "He kills blonde cheerleaders."

It was my junior year, and like most fall Fridays, we were decked out in our cheerleading uniforms: short skirt, tight V-neck tank tops, knee-length socks, and matching shoes. My eyes darted to the guy they were talking about, standing a few feet away at his locker. I kept walking and sighed to myself. I slammed my locker shut. *I'm done with this rumor,* I thought. *It seems ridiculous. Seriously?*

AN EMOTIONALLY RESONATING STORY DOESN'T MEAN IT'S A TRUE ONE

I look back now and realize why I was frustrated. I seemed to be the only one who questioned this "common truth." Others were reveling in it.

I felt like an "odd" high school student—always a part of the popular crowd yet gravitating toward those who seemed the least bit "different." At our country school, Jacob was a guy who stood out as interesting. And I appreciated his difference and felt protective over him.

At lunch, all the girls were chatting about it. According to the cheerleading team, this guy was a "confirmed Satanist."

I piped up after ten minutes of listening. "How do we know he is a Satanist?"

One of the other cheerleaders answered with the so-called truth and spoke slowly as if I were a little hard of hearing. "He admitted it. Jackie and I asked him if he enjoyed killing blonde cheerleaders and he said, 'Yes, it's my favorite thing to do.' We both ran away and immediately told Mr. Taylor."

As I looked closely at this cheerleader, it hit me that her hair was in fact, not blonde, but instead a permed mousy brown. I wanted to point out she didn't need to be concerned since she did not have blonde hair—but it felt too obvious.

Just then, I remembered a couple of days prior a prayer group started at our church for the "murders" occurring in nearby small towns. Mostly cows had been murdered, but there were insinuations that possibly humans could be next. I had shivered then. It made me feel anxious and fearful. It hit me that fear that could spread like wildfire, especially when the stories tap into our greatest fears.

DISCOVERY REQUIRES INTERNAL REFLECTION, OBSERVATION, AND WILLINGNESS TO BE WRONG

I got up to refill my coke, threw away the now-soggy cafeteria nachos, and made my way slowly to class, contemplating the situation. Yes, it was exciting to think something dangerous was going on in this school besides the norm, albeit morbid.

I sat down in Social Studies, trying to shake off the rumor, questioning my own judgment. I decided to observe him a little closer while I reflected on the situation. Something didn't seem right, and I could not decide if it was them or me who had incorrect thinking.

Jacob sat down behind me to my right. Until that day, I had not actively talk to him. But I was focused on him now and observed his shyness. Compared to the other boys cutting up with one another, I realized, he seemed respectful and kind. That was the incongruence I had experienced in their story.

I remembered he would let me borrow his pen if I forgot mine. One time, I had drifted off, then whispered to him frantically, "What did she tell us to do?" And he whispered back just as discreetly how to get back on track.

But after the bell rang, I soon forgot about Jacob or the supposed dead blonde girls in his wake.

Much later, I was one of the last to leave after the pep rally. As I walked toward my car, I saw Jacob sitting by himself on the edge of the curb between the lawn and school driveway. He was reading a book, his Social Studies book. The same one I had yet to open.

DISCOVERY HELPS VALIDATE OR INVALIDATE THE STATUS QUO

I decided I would discover for myself. Since the news had been primarily focused on the gory, evil things people were doing to each other, I noticed how hard it was to focus. I felt anxious to talk to him, but I also was curious about him.

So, I moved toward instead of away from him. It must have been startling because he looked up quickly, shutting the book. I said, "Mind if I sit down with you?"

His eyes widened and he said, "Sure."

"So how was your day? I asked.

He breathed deeply and let out a large exhale. "It was okay. I am trying to study now because when I get home, I'll have to get dinner ready for my brother and do the week's laundry. Most of the weekend is full with work for my dad, and I won't have time to study before Monday."

"Wow!" I exclaimed. "You are dedicated. That's surprising."

He smiled. "Why are you surprised?"

"Oh, I don't know," I answered. And then in the next moment, I asked, "What are you still doing here?"

He responded, "My ride's not here yet."

"When is it coming?"

"I'm not sure. I thought my dad was coming after school, but he hasn't yet."

I looked at my watch, knowing I needed to get ready for tonight's game. But then I said, "Would you mind if I sat and waited with you?"

He said, "Sure. I would love that."

EMPATHIC DISCOVERY REQUIRES SPACE AND TIME INVESTMENT

For the next thirty minutes, we chatted—about life, high school, and most of all, loneliness. He told me how his mom had left when he was young. Then he became the "man of the house," taking care of his two younger siblings. He described what happened when he did not do it as carefully as expected.

He said, "I wish someone understood me, but I feel judged because I look different. I feel like an outcast. Like I don't belong."

My eyes welled up a bit and I said, "I know how you feel."

"No way you could feel lonely. You are a cheerleader," he proclaimed, "with friends always surrounding you."

And my reply was simple. "I don't think any of us are spared loneliness."

Then he looked me in the eyes for the second time that day. And as I looked back at him, I knew that he knew I knew what was being said about him.

He looked down with shame and said, "Yeah, but you don't say things on purpose to keep people away."

I realized in that moment it doesn't take much for a proclaimed belief to spread like wildfire. It takes a lot more intentional listening, time, and willingness to discover with empathy.

IT'S NOT WHAT YOU ASK, IT'S WHO YOU'RE BEING WHEN YOU ASK

I understood why the rumors about him had come to life. He told me the story of being approached with demanding questions. They had barraged him with their inquisition, determined to get answers about his presumed killing spree. And he chose an answer that had fueled the rumor.

Instead of defending himself, he had replied to their questions with, "Yeah, so what of it?"

Confused and curious at his incongruency, I asked, "Well, why are you telling me a different story?"

He said, "You seem like you really want to know who I am, rather than what I'm capable of. Who I am is a guy trying to survive being lonely through high school until I can get out from under my dad."

DISCOVER FROM THOSE WHOSE OPINIONS MATTER TO YOU

Jacob never knew the impact he had on me. I learned to trust my own curiosity and seek to understand a greater truth than the common one.

I also learned what it meant to seek the truth of being human that day. And that we all have emotions, and emotions can trigger behaviors that create chaos.

I realized the beauty in understanding the truth of someone who was not like me.

And mostly, he clarified whose opinion mattered to me.

Sometimes the biggest challenge in our innovation journey is to declutter all of the voices that do not matter and find ones that do. Every good product innovator or marketer knows that creating for everyone is creating for no one. We create for those we care most about. That day, I learned how much I cared about the outliers, the ones whose voices are quieter, the ones who have something to say but are a little "abnormal," often misunderstood. They were the most like me.

TRUTHS DISCOVERED FROM EMOTIONAL CONNECTION CAN DEBUNK "COMMON TRUTHS"

In the spirit of innovation, I decided to create a new story with my new truth. By discovering shared truth of loneliness with Jacob, I could see another way to handle the rumors.

The next Monday, I knew a new truth—something others did not because they had not taken the time to discover like I had. I had a broader perspective.

I whispered in every gossiping ear I could find that I had taken Jacob home on Friday between the pep rally and game in my car, alone. The gasps and horrified looks were so fun as I walked away. I tossed my long, curly red hair over my shoulder with a smile, saying, "Well, I thought I was safe because I have red hair. Turns out I was right."

The rumors about his killing spree died off soon afterward. They didn't have the flame they once had.

It was worth the risk to look beyond widely held opinions.

DISCOVERING WITH EMPATHY CREATES TRANSFORMATIVE CHANGE

The reason for discovering with empathy to create change is because it forges a path toward greater truth, a truth that is connected between people's separate truths, and between the logic of the mind and the connected emotions of the heart.

Sometimes we can only clear out the loud voices in our heads by listening through the heart of another.

When you're willing to look underneath the cover, there's a world of possibility.

When we don't know 100 percent, when the data can't tell us everything, the best thing to do before starting to create anything is to take some space, understand what you know and what still needs to be learned, then spark a fire from shared truth.

FIRESTARTER SPARKS—EMPATHY HELPS YOU EXPAND KNOWLEDGE BY LISTENING TO LEARN

1. Strategy Doesn't Lead to Learning, Learning Leads to Strategy
2. Discovering Emotional Desires & Challenges Disrupts False Beliefs
3. Listening to Learn is Contagious
4. Solving problems with current perspective defeats the Point of Innovation
5. Discovering with Empathy Creates Exponential Possibility
6. Perspective-Taking Builds a Bridge, Empathy Crosses It
7. Discovery Helps us Better Understand "Common Truths"
8. An Emotionally Resonating Story Doesn't Mean It's a True One
9. Discovery Requires Internal Reflection, Observation and Willingness to Be Wrong
10. Discovery Helps Validate or Invalidate the Status Quo

11. Empathic Discovery Requires Space and Time Investment
12. It's Not What You Ask, It's Who You're Being When You Ask
13. Discover from Those Whose Opinions Matter To You
14. Truths Discovered from Emotional Connection Can Debunk "Common Truths"
15. Discovering with Empathy Creates Transformative Change

FIRESTARTER FUEL—IGNITING ME

1. What do you wonder or wish you knew more about?
2. What do you already know to be true?
3. Who do you want to learn more from?
4. Who could help you see a different perspective?
5. For whom do you currently have no empathy, but want to understand better?

FIRESTARTER FUEL—IGNITING WE

1. What does your team constantly argue about?
2. Where are other team members coming from that you can't see?
3. Regarding the most difficult person on the team: What keeps this person up at night that you don't know about?
4. What do you believe to be true about each member on your team?

CHAPTER 4

DISCERN

It was a bright, sunny day in Dallas. My roommate and I were chatting on our fourth-floor uptown apartment balcony, which overlooked downtown Dallas. We lived in a newly built, chic apartment building, amongst others like us enjoying the riches of a single professional life. My roommate was a friend since college, like a brother. I was twenty-eight, and it felt like the world was my oyster: we had money to spend, free time on our hands outside of jobs we loved, a well-connected group of friends. It was a happy time.

A few months before, I had reconnected with a guy who went on the same international exchange program back in college. I can't remember what country he went to, but we met in DC during the introduction program, just before we all flew off to our distinct countries. Our connection, at that point, was just a quick spark. But considering when and how we met, it never really went beyond a raised eyebrow type of interest. We kept in touch. In those days it was handwritten letters.

Then one day he called, and over the course of a few conversations, we began the process of discovering more about each other. He shared his struggles, including the challenges he was having at work, and that he felt stuck in his very small town. Working for the forestry service did not lend him much in the way of connecting with others, and he felt the itch to make a "fresh start." This emotionally connected with me, because I had been where he was, stuck in a small town with an unfulfilling job just before taking my current one. Even though now I was in a different place, I could easily empathize. So, one day, on impulse, I suggested he come visit and "see what Dallas is like as a possibility for your future."

And not long after, he made his way from his small town near St. Louis to Dallas.

ACTING BEFORE DISCERNING CAN LEAD US ASTRAY

I was shocked when he showed up at my doorstep, on a bright spring morning, with two bags and a large cardboard box. I was not expecting that. I reflected on our conversation, playing it back in my mind. I knew I had not asked him to "move to Dallas." And then it hit me— we had not discussed how long he would stay. I had just replied, *"Great, here's my address."*

As I looked at him in dismay standing at my door with his belongings, I didn't understand that him coming meant he was going to be sleeping on our living room couch for an indefinite amount of time. I realized a lot of details that were left unsaid. I wish he had been clear on three important ones before giving him my address:

1. I'm planning to move to Dallas
2. I'm planning to move in with you
3. I'm coming without a job

This was a key moment for me, one that not only interrupted the lively conversation my roommate and I were having, but also interrupted my life.

I also did not understand that joining him would be a box of earthworms intended to help my roommate and I compost our food as they rummaged around underneath our kitchen sink.

It did not take long until I noticed other parts of my life of complete freedom and joy shift.

WITHOUT PROPER DISCERNMENT WE CAN WASTE TIME SOLVING THE WRONG PROBLEM

I could see it was time to fix his other problem (finding a job) and in my haste to solve it, I helped him get a job at the company where I worked. He even got a job in the same department as me. That proved to be another not-well-thought-out decision. Not only was this guy sleeping on my couch, but now he was in my space at work. There's something about a revived spark that tends to die down quickly when the things you're enjoying in your life begin to be overtaken without enough space between two people.

The attraction I initially felt when we reconnected quickly shifted. I suddenly felt responsible for his well-being, financial state, and living arrangements. Attraction was replaced with a consistent, low-grade guilt and, eventually, resentment.

I found myself making decisions based on him, instead of me. I began to forget what I enjoyed and instead focused on whether he felt good. For example, I wasn't ready to date him exclusively. I wanted to date others. But it was challenging to go out with another date when he was sitting on my couch, eating my food, and watching my TV.

I remember one night a few friends decided to go out dancing. We had a group of five girls and three guys, including my roommate and him. We were at a bar with several dance rooms. We danced in each room for a while, before skipping to the next with a new band or a new beat. In addition to rotating rooms, we also changed dance partners. I remember him trying to hold my hand as we migrated through the different rooms, and I kept taking my hand back. I felt chained, weighed down. That was a tipping point.

About the third time it happened, he got mad at me, threw my hand down, and stomped out of the club. I attempted to dance a little longer, but our drama became clear to my friends. Either out of amazing kindness or sheer curiosity, they helped me locate him. Unfortunately, it took some time as we walked the crowded streets and bars in the East Dallas neighborhood, people buzzing everywhere.

We continued the search, and thirty minutes later, found him sulking at a CVS parking lot.

When we got home, my poor roommate listened to the fight that ensued in the next room. Nothing I could do would console him, and the anger and resentment I had been suppressing came out. I was so frustrated at having to end the night with my friends early because he was mad at me for not holding his hand. I realized we were in a bind because it would no longer work for him to sleep on the couch. I had lost interest in continuing to even casually date him, but he was now working at my company, and I would see him every day regardless.

DISCERNMENT REQUIRES SLOWING DOWN

The next day after the air cleared, he said he was going to take a quick trip. I exhaled. When he returned, we were both ready to sit down and talk.

He started with, "I think I needed to slow down before just showing up on your doorstep. I acted on impulse and can see that while I wanted it to be a good surprise, maybe it was a little much." I smiled at him, appreciating his insight and acknowledgment.

And then I reciprocated the generosity. "Well, I'm the one who just said, 'come on down' without us really talking about what we wanted."

As we openly talked about what we had learned about each other and what we individually desired, it was clear we had to make a shift. We eventually worked out the details and logistics to move both him and his earthworms out. And we decided that since we worked together a friendship was best for the time being. Eventually, he moved on and away from Dallas.

DISCERNING WITH EMPATHY ALLOWS US TO SEPARATE OUR EMOTION FROM OTHERS

What I realize now is that in my process of discovery, I did not pause to connect with my own desire. Instead, I got emotionally swept up into a situation that took a lot of untangling. What I needed was better discernment. If I had slowed down from our initial phone conversations, reflecting and seeing where our desires were aligned and where they were not, it would have served us both better.

Going into anything new—whether it's a relationship or creating an innovative solution, service, or product—it is more productive for the long-term to pause between emotional connection and creating next steps.

Otherwise, if you move straight from discovery into designing or creating, you can get emotionally tied to one outcome. And that leads to spending energy and effort down a path that doesn't serve your initial desire. Most of what we emotionally resonate with when we're discovering are the things that most relate to what we already know or believe to be true. So, stepping back and looking at patterns allows us to see things more holistically.

This is where understanding the role of empathy is paramount, specifically empathic reflection. Most people believe that empathy equals the ability to be with strong emotions, but there's another useful element to empathy: empathic reflection. Empathic reflection is a purposeful action of thinking and drawing meaning from it (Salem, 2021) And it is helpful when discerning because it helps us be with emotion without getting caught up in it. When we get caught up in emotion, this is called emotional contagion. Emotional contagion is when we experience other's emotions that lead to reflexive behavior (Neuroscience & Biobehavioral Reviews, 2019).

Instead, empathic reflection involves paying attention to both the content of what is being said as well as the feelings associated (Empathetic Reflection, 2021).

DISCERNMENT IS LOOKING FOR PATTERNS

Discernment is the most overlooked step when innovating because our instinct is to go straight to solving. But often, when we focus on the solution, we won't see the patterns. When disparate information comes together, our brains need time to process and assimilate new information and to integrate it. The patterns are what gives us the ability to connect disassociated ideas and create from those. Analyzing data is often thought of when looking at numerical data but it is even more important to analyze and define emotional data.

Allowing room to discern through reflective listening using pattern recognition is a skill that helps every time you are trying to create a path in the unknown. Because empathic reflective listening overcomes confirmation bias, allowing for our brains to expand.

That includes looking holistically at what is discovered. The way we do this in our innovation projects is to debrief our learnings after each discovery encounter, allowing our brain to process what was learned without trying to solve for it. Over time, these singular instances of understanding emotions can begin to develop themes. Themes become a driver for broader, larger stories grounded in truth. When you're grounded in the truth of desire, you can solve in a more meaningful way, one that sticks.

I have seen this work time after time, but one project resonates with me of the value of discernment by defining patterns.

I received a text message from my client one Saturday afternoon while driving my daughter from one activity to the next. Her text said, "Do you have a few minutes for a quick chat about next week's project?"

Minutes later, we arrived at the birthday party, and after doing my hello rounds, I asked another mom to keep an eye on my daughter, jumped back into my car and replied, "Yes, I do now." She called.

As we began chatting, I could hear her concern. "We have a lot of disagreement over the designs we're testing next week. One leader in upper management is set on one, the agency is convinced of another and the rest of us still want to see improvement on them all. We really want to know what our consumer thinks so we can evolve."

I listened carefully then said, "Yes, I don't think we'll have a problem. We do this all the time. I can get you this learning."

"Wait, there's more. We've had someone else step in at the last hour. They are convinced we are not even on the right track. They want us to do a discovery exercise before we begin testing the designs because she doesn't think our concepts fit with our brand."

I exhaled deeply. "Okay, tell me more."

She went on to tell me about the variations they were considering testing and why. We ended the conversation with a plan to get everyone on the same page before we started the discovery interviews.

When we began the project the following week, I could have cut through the tension in the air with a knife. Everyone was on edge. But we started the conversation at a high level with their desire. The conversation was passionate, and they were able to align on a common goal even with individual preferences.

And then I asked: "Would the team be okay if we 'debrief' our learnings after each interview?"

This is my term for verbal empathic reflection conducted with a flip chart and markers where we "data dump" what we hear: surprises, validations, interesting quotes, etc.

One of the marketing leaders piped up and said honestly, *"I really think that's a waste of time. It's literally one person at a time we're talking to, we can't make a decision after talking to one person."*

DISCERNING IS NOT THE SAME AS DECIDING

I acknowledged the concern, agreeing that decision-making could not happen effectively until much later. But I added at length, "The value of debriefing allows our brains to integrate and layer upon what we learn. And when we go back after hearing twelve interviews, we are better able to assess and make sense of the patterns than if we waited until after all interviews are over. At that point, it will be more challenging to distinctly see the patterns because we will be so tired from our active listening.

"What I've seen with a team of tired brains who have been actively listening for three to four days to one-on-one interviews is that we can confuse data if we are not constantly debriefing to see patterns. My job is for you to individually learn, but also create patterns together rather than rely on common individual bias."

Heads nodded in agreement. So I went on. "Our brains are wired to want to remember what we are most attached to. But we can combat emotional or cognitive bias through repetitive acknowledgment or reflection on what we're hearing before we decide."

And so we began.

After the first four interviews, we understood that one of the five designs was clearly in the lead. It emotionally resonated and we understood why.

Then suddenly, on interview five, an almost opposite view was explained thoroughly. Then the next two interviews had mixed emotional reactions to the designs. Many teams get frustrated with conflicting learnings and the challenge of weaving together complex human opinions and emotions. But this team, even with their differences, had committed to an empathic and reflective regurgitation process.

SEPARATING DATA TO LOOK AT IT IN NEW WAYS HELPS US DISCERN

I was pleased as their initial confusion gave way to greater understanding. At about the eighth interview, three of the team members began using these insights to develop a more robust approach that had not been considered before. Suddenly, we could all see how three of the designs could transform and evolve into something new and possibly in multiple ways as a combination of what had not been working with the originals.

So, instead of a linear one-dimensional way of looking at the problem with the question of deciding "which design wins," they moved through the innovation journey and forged a path which ultimately created much better designs for the product package.

Fast forward three years later, one of the package design ideas from this project was eventually executed and made its way to the shelf. It did exponentially better than expected, so much so that their biggest problem was how to keep it stocked. Further, this product lifted their brand's market share by 65 percent in their category the year it was released.

While this was not the only component that increased their success rate, it was their ability as a team to contribute and listen to learn together, which helped them navigate as they continued down the journey to bring the product to life.

When we start connecting deeply, it's easy for us to act fast because we are driven emotionally as we connect to a greater need. And yet, we are equally connected to our own views and beliefs about what we are trying to create. But acting slowly is a better approach when innovating because there are myriad ways to use discovery data to innovate for emotionally resonating creations.

FIRESTARTER SPARKS—EMPATHY HELPS DISCERN EMOTIONAL PATTERNS AND CONNECT THE DOTS

1. Acting Before Discerning Can Lead Us Astray
2. Without Proper Discernment We Can Waste Time Solving the Wrong Problem

3. Discernment Requires Slowing Down
4. Discerning with Empathy Allows Us to Separate Our Emotion from Others
5. Discernment is Looking for Patterns
6. Discerning is Not the Same as Deciding
7. Separating Data to Look at It in New Ways Helps Us Discern

FIRESTARTER FUEL—IGNITING ME

1. What did you learn from this discovery that matters most to your original desire/vision?
2. What are the key patterns you saw throughout the discovery process?
3. What are the biggest emotional challenges or problems to solve?
4. What problem do you want to, and have a unique capacity/capability to solve?
5. How would you piece together these learnings in larger "buckets" based on the themes?

FIRESTARTER FUEL—IGNITING WE

1. What are we learning that either confirms or invalidates our original bias?
2. What are the primary "truths" we all agree on?
3. What is the impact of these learnings on each member of the team?
4. What do we as a team believe now that we have integrated this new learning?

CHAPTER 5

DESIGN

I walked into the room full of clients, fresh off my flight. We were meeting at their "Idea Incubator" lab. It was my second project with this specific team. A few months earlier, we had completed extensive research to understand consumer appeal for a chemical-free bug repellent. While this may seem like a no-brainer today, it was mid-2000—before DEET-free products had been brought to market en masse.

I love working with the same teams on different projects. Not only do I learn their capabilities to better help them succeed, but I also get to hear the results of our former work. I was accustomed to teams showing me how our work had grown from a "tiny seed" of an idea into product form. Most of the time, at least one idea we tested would move into some form of development. Eventually, I, along with millions of others, would see it packaged on a shelf in a store. That feels like success to me.

So, I was surprised at their answer when I asked how the ideas for their chemical-free bug repellent product line were doing. One guy smiled widely and said, "Oh, thanks for asking. Those are a no-go. They went into our 'Failed It' bin."

I sharply inhaled. "Oh no," I exclaimed, wondering whether to ask more. I was anxious and confused. My mind scrambled to understand why they were smiling, given that everything we designed and tested had failed. And yet, here I was, with them again, being paid to do similar work with a new product category. I secretly wondered why they had hired me a second time when everything we spent months working on had failed.

And then he said something I will never forget. "You do know one of our KPIs is to fail a certain number of product ideas each quarter, don't you?"

"What?" I was shocked. "No, I didn't realize that."

And my mind raced back to the work, money, and time we invested to deeply understand consumers' desires around chemical-free insect repellents. Our goal to learn everything we could led us to discover what moms wanted for themselves and their kids. We observed them using bug spray, listened to conversations, joined them at outdoor events, and eventually discerned patterns.

We learned there were plenty of frustrations regarding product form, color, consistency, and application process. But we also recognized a pattern that consumers did not believe it would be possible to "get rid of bugs" without DEET or heavy chemicals. "Organic" wasn't a word tossed around at that time and neither was "DEET-free."

DESIGNING FOR EMOTIONAL RESONANCE IS MORE IMPACTFUL THAN DESIGNING FOR FORM

While consumers desired "natural" in products, they had a bigger emotional need: "Keep me and my family safe and protected from bugs... no matter how it is done."

So, when we created ideas on paper for chemical-free products, we noticed consumers resonated with the product forms (wrist bracelets, soaps, shampoos, hanging lights) more than the emotional experience. But the point of the project was to introduce chemical-free repellants whereas they struggled to connect with the idea of a DEET-free repellant.

Once these ideas went into test with a larger audience, the discoveries from our initial findings remained true: they simply did not believe a repellent could do both—be chemical-free and deliver on safety. The team was ahead of their time.

FAILING IS A CRITICAL COMPONENT OF THE DESIGN PROCESS

"Why do you have a goal to fail? That doesn't seem right to me. I'm confused." I asked the marketing leader.

He described two reasons:

1. Innovation must include making room for failure.
2. If we make room to embrace instead of reject failure, the products we eventually launch will be better.

Still perplexed, I continued to press, even though I knew he was anxious to start our new project. He realized I wanted to make sense of it so paused for me to explain why embracing failure was beneficial.

He said, "The process was designed to succeed by reframing failure as a path to success.

It's kind of like drinking water from a glass rather than a firehose. If they tried to launch every idea they thought of, it wouldn't be possible to operationalize, systemize, and maintain products in a sustainable way. So, by reframing failure, it helps maintain the team's brilliance at creating."

OUR IDEAS EXPAND WHEN WE ARE NOT AFRAID TO FAIL

That wasn't all. He went on, saying, "Embracing failure helps us continue to innovate and develop ideas while still leaving room for the company to sustainably operate."

"In fact," he said, "failure helps us continue to generate new ideas. That's why the company appreciates the failure. They know the less likely we are to worry about failing, the more and, eventually, better ideas we will generate.

"Besides," he said in a whisper, "Give it ten years. That chemical-free repellant we created, especially the one for kids will become a winner. I bet it will sell like hotcakes!" He winked.

Most of us, in our drive to succeed, fear failure. Ironically, when we are afraid to fail, we will not take the necessary risks to truly innovate. But allowing our brains to live in possibility without fear of failure enhances the brain's ability to create possibility.

According to *Psychology Today* in their article: "Why Fear of Failure Can Keep You Stuck," they elaborate on the deep meaning we put on failing, including the belief that we "don't have what it takes," we become "irrelevant," we are "letting people down," and ultimately we "have a lot to lose." While we as a human species have survived by using our fear, we were not all born with a fear of failure. We were raised with it. We fear failure because we are taught to avoid it, we learn to not fail in our homes, schools, our sports, and other activities.

Further, as we grow up, we continue to be rewarded for producing results. It is normal to "get ahead" in an organization for having good ideas. Who wants to be associated with a bad idea? It's usually safer to keep a project going and hope for the best rather than to be associated with a "failed idea." Because of this common fear of failure, organizations often inhibit bringing the best designs to the table for exploration when innovating, and instead, opt only for the ones they believe will succeed.

DESIGNING REQUIRES A SPIRIT OF EXPERIMENTATION

Embracing failure is easier if you perceive it as an experiment.

If failure was defined as an experimental way of learning rather than something to fear, innovation would change. According to *Harvard Business Review* in their article: "The No. 1 Enemy of Creativity: Fear of Failure", many companies are adopting a mindset that allows failure to be a part of the design process. They mentioned several leaders at companies like Amazon, Pixar, GE, Procter & Gamble, General Mills, and Clorox who make it cool to be imperfect at the early stages of new projects. Bill Hewlett, cofounder of Hewlett Packard, calls it "small bet" innovation and has created formulas to predict wins—"100 small bets to find 6 breakthroughs."

When we can view failure with an experimental lens like this, our imagination is activated because we center our heart back to desire and focus on discovering emotional truths, then discern patterns and solving for them without fear of failing getting in the way.

It also helps us stay open to possibility especially when we are connected empathetically with the user we are designing for.

DESIGNING WITH EMPATHY CREATES ALCHEMY

To move original designs to successful innovations, the designs must be tested to understand what emotionally connects with the user. Many of the most phenomenal innovations have been due to an innovator's willingness to "follow the user" while designing:

- Viagra was originally designed to lower blood pressure
- Play-Doh was originally used as a wallpaper cleaner
- Listerine was originally designed as an antiseptic
- Febreze was originally designed only for those who smoke or had pets

Design is about possibility, but not every possibility has to be "the winner." Great innovations are about what "emotionally sticks." Just like these brands, the original idea was one possibility but as they observed users experiencing their initial ideas, something else "emotionally resonated." By empathizing with the user, "alchemy" occurred.

The definition of "alchemy" according to Merriam-Webster dictionary is: "a power or process that changes or transforms something in a mysterious or impressive way."

Another definition by Oxford Languages defines it as a "seemingly magical process of transformation, creation, or combination."

Rory Sutherland, Vice Chairman of Ogilvy UK, in his book, Alchemy, says it best: "When you demand logic, you pay a hidden price, you destroy magic." He goes on to say, "If we allow the world to be run by logical people, we will only discover logical things. But in real life, most things aren't logical—they are psycho-logical."

Alchemy is created when the innovator discovers something in their designs by going beyond what logically makes sense to them. That is what happened on the north side of Chicago during an innovation project where we were experimenting with initial prototypes (designs) for frozen appetizers.

TESTING MAKES GOOD DESIGNS GREAT

When my three clients and I pulled up to the three-story brownstone, I immediately sensed a problem: there were no cars. I expected to see at least three or four because we had recruited consumers to invite friends over for a house party to help us "test" these appetizer prototypes.

This was our third phase of the innovation project. We had come to observe users to understand their reactions to the newly-designed frozen appetizers the team had shipped to their homes the week before.

I knocked on the door. Suddenly, I noticed a flicker in my peripheral vision out of the corner of my left eye. I glanced over and saw an eye peeking through an opening in the slat of blinds. Then quickly, the blinds shut as the eye caught mine, blinked, and disappeared.

My attention was directed back toward the door. An elderly lady around the age of seventy opened it, out of breath. She seemed to not know we were coming. Confused, I looked down at the paper in my hands, at the summary of respondent details: male, age thirty-two. We had recruited him to invite two to four friends. I asked politely if this was the home of Patrick.

Out of the corner of my left eye, I saw another movement likely from the lower basement window. I heard
someone walking slowly up the stairs, from the basement
within the house. And then I saw him, short man, slightly
overweight, balding, who looked to be forty-five escorted
us in, brushing his mother out of the way.

These clients were a good bunch. Jovial, fun, great sense
of humor, with a leader who demonstrated an empathic
innovative spirit. Even still, my heart sank as we entered
the house. Our previous few days of testing the product
designs had been great. We learned so much about which
appetizers resonated based on who they were serving.

As we entered the hallway, we could see the kitchen off
to the right. The lights were so low that I wasn't sure, but
it did not seem there were additional guests in the home,
as we had instructed.

It was my job to create immediate connection and comfort so that both my clients and the respondent could
ease into letting strangers be a part of an intimate social
gathering. So, I breathed in deeply and asked, "So, Patrick,
tell me a little about the party or social gathering you
were planning today."

He spoke shyly. "Well, I know you wanted me to invite
more people, but my friend who I usually get together
with for football and apps didn't want to come. I usually go over to his house; he doesn't come here." He side-
glanced toward his mom.

"Oh, I understand," I said, accepting this would be a different kind of gathering than what we had expected. As I glanced at the team, I wondered how long I had before they would be anxious to leave. I knew to glance up at them occasionally, and they would eventually signal me when it was time. I half-hoped it would be now. Instead, I set in for what I knew would be a tougher interview than most.

Forty minutes later, after watching a football game with Patrick sitting between him and his mom, while eating several of the frozen appetizers we had sent him, I didn't think there was anything else left to ask. As he got up to grab something from the kitchen, I looked at the team expectantly and as assumed, they were ready to go.

As Patrick entered the room, we were all getting up from the couch to leave until I saw what he was carrying. "Patrick, it's been so great to—" I stopped mid-sentence.

DESIGN ADAPTATION CAN CREATE MASTERPIECES

He was carrying a tray of warmed-up pizza rolls...

I was shocked because we had specifically asked our users to only prepare the appetizers we sent. Everyone else had complied. But he clearly danced to his own beat. When consumers do something unusual during a design test, sometimes it can be a golden opportunity. This was one of those days. My clients sat back down as I asked, "Patrick, do you mind sharing why you prepared these appetizers?

They seem very different than the ones we shipped you to test."

He looked surprised by my question and said, "Well, after eating the ones you sent, I started craving these pizza rolls. I always have them on hand because I love them.

I would eat them all day, every day if I could."

The team sat still. One started taking notes. So, I kept asking questions, waiting for the team's cues to leave, not knowing if they were making a note to never use me again as a resource since I obviously couldn't get respondents to comply with instructions or if they were interested in what he was saying.

My questioning led to Patrick telling us about how pizza rolls created an "indulgent comfort" and a "mental break from his mom." I asked him to compare the attributes of the appetizers we had sent him against the pizza rolls to learn more of what was missing in the new prototypes that created the comfort pizza rolls gave him.

DESIGNING WITH EMPATHY REQUIRES LETTING GO OF OLD ASSUMPTIONS

As we climbed back into our large vehicle, I felt anxious—nervous about what the client's takeaway from the respondent had been. It was not often that an unusual respondent turned out to be insightful.

I had been trained to always ask the clients, "Okay what did we learn?" So, when I asked and heard the answer, I exhaled a breath of relief after the leader piped up first.

He said he had learned:

1. I'm glad I moved out of my mom's house when I did
2. This process is a little bit like digging for gold—sometimes you find it and sometimes you don't and...
3. We found gold.

He went on, saying, "We started with an incorrect assumption based on historical sales data that appetizers were primarily for social purposes to 'create connection.' All of our designs were created with that in mind. But we missed something. We have an opportunity to 'create indulgent comfort.' We were thinking too narrow."

The team's perspective had broadened in the middle of a brownstone home in Chicago with a lonely forty-five-year-old guy who lived with his mom, finding a way to justify his frozen appetizer consumption. Empathy had not only allowed the team to relate to Patrick but also to build other possibilities for appetizer usage.

When the team listened empathically to something they did not formerly understand, they were able to design from a broader perspective. That team went on to tweak the design that resonated the most by adding a melty cheese to it, and now that product is still a bestseller in the category. Eventually, they expanded the line to include appetizers marketed for individual consumption only.

My own journey of "innovating with empathy" has been challenged with old assumptions. I wrongly assumed that women would be more interested in innovating with "empathy" than men. In fact, when I first began my "empathy interviews" for this book, I expected to interview women. I had many try to tell me to think bigger, but I was stuck in my beliefs. But once I decided to listen to what others kept telling me, my view broadened, with one email request asking leaders to join my study, I over-indexed exponentially with male leaders interested. What a lesson on empathy for me! Once I became open to rethinking my old beliefs, it altered the course of how I have brought my own ideas to life. It is so much better than I could have imagined.

FIRESTARTER SPARKS—EMPATHY HELPS YOU IDEATE AND CREATE PASSION-LED POSSIBILITIES
1. Designing for Emotional Resonance is More Impactful than Designing for Form
2. Failing is a Critical Component of the Design Process
3. Our Ideas Expand When We Are Not Afraid to Fail
4. Designing Requires a Spirit of Experimentation
5. Designing with Empathy Creates Alchemy
6. Testing Makes Good Designs Great
7. Design Adaptation Can Create Masterpieces
8. Designing with Empathy Requires Letting Go of Old Assumptions

FIRESTARTER FUEL—IGNITING ME

1. What would you try to create if you were to embrace the idea of failure?
2. What would you design if it were a game so that failure was incorporated, accepted, and appreciated for the gift that it is?
3. What beliefs do you currently have about what is possible for your life and what is not?

FIRESTARTER FUEL—IGNITING WE

1. Where is it not okay to fail in our organization?
2. In what small ways can our team experiment with new ideas allowing room to fail incrementally?
3. What are the boundaries for what is acceptable and unacceptable to create or design? Who owns these boundaries? Why are they there?

CHAPTER 6

DECIDE

Sometimes, you begin an innovation journey knowing the framework upon which you will base your decision. But sometimes, innovation takes you to better and bigger places than you ever thought possible. That is what happened when I decided to experiment with innovating in my own life. I want to invite you into decision-making so you can see the magic, the alchemy of innovating with empathy by letting the process help you decide.

DECISIONS BECOME CLEAR WHEN YOU FOLLOW THE PROCESS

We sat on her bed in the pitch dark. There were no curtains on the bay windows of her bedroom. The lamp was on the floor, her boxes piled high along the wall next to the door. The quiet of our new home was almost deafening. It was a little after 10:00 p.m. As we sat together, our breathing slowed, and so did my mind. I could hear the cicadas, their rhythm intense, the loud droning cutting through the quiet of the two-plus acres we moved into that day, my daughter and I.

In the dark, sleepily, she said the words I didn't even know I had been looking for. "Mom, have you ever felt like you just came home for the first time?" My tears welled and spilled over, one sliding down my cheek. I sucked in for a larger breath, willing myself not to cry. I quickly wiped the tear that managed to escape, keeping my composure.

Breathing deeply, knowing how she felt, I said, "Yes, honey. I do know how that feels."

She looked up at me, searching. "That's how I feel tonight."

I exhaled. "Me too. Thank you for sharing that with me."

We hugged for a good thirty seconds. I will never forget that hug. It had so many meanings wrapped into it, relief for arriving, grief for all we had been through to get here, emotional, physical, and mental exhaustion, expectancy for what was to come, joy in having each other, expectancy in the unknown. All in one hug.

I walked outside onto the pasture. The two beautiful quarter horses, a dapple gray and a bay were quietly grazing along the fence between the pool and the pasture.

I can't believe they came with the house, I thought to myself as I walked out beyond the barn barefoot, venturing toward the sand horse arena toward the back of the property, enjoying the softness on my feet. The creek was running along the property's perimeter. When I looked up, I saw a sky full of stars and the sliver of a crescent moon. I exhaled again, hardly believing what the last four months had entailed.

Our journey to innovate my daughter's education began the second week of January when I committed to it. My desire, after attending a conference the week before, was to better understand what would help Autumn thrive holistically (socially, emotionally, mentally, and physically). We were only six months outside of the divorce and had received Autumn's ADHD diagnosis after a teacher prompted us to have her tested.

Autumn did not want to change schools. I understood that. She had seen enough change with our divorce. And yet, I knew what she did not. Her life at this Montessori school was about to change drastically as she moved into fourth grade. The class of twenty-four students would double in size. Her best friend would not be moving up with her. And I intuitively questioned the school's ability to meet her where she was given her recent diagnosis. I decided to use the process I knew well to innovate with empathy, whether we changed schools or not.

Discovering the "perfect" school fit in Dallas is like finding "the perfect swimsuit" when you're in your mid-forties. There are *a lot* of options yet finding the "right one" for you can be tricky. From reputation, distance, private or public, qualifications, specialties for learning styles, there were as many options for schools as nail salons.

I asked if she was willing to experiment with me "just to learn" so we agreed upon a common desire "to discover if our current school was the best option going forward or if there was a better alternative." Her father concurred. She was convinced her current school was the best option, but I was not. We differed, but we both agreed if we stuck to the common goal and allowed ourselves to be open, it would be a win/win.

DECIDING IS EASIER WHEN YOU BEGIN WITH HEART-LEAD DESIRE

So, we created a "Discovery Grid" out of a large white foam board to help us better visualize the data. It was six feet long by four feet wide. She created "gridlines" out of washi tape of her choosing. On the left column, we created our "criteria" which included:

• Date of exploration
• Cost
• Best thing
• Biggest concern or challenge
• Autumn's overall feelings (smile, neutral, or frown)
• April's overall feelings (smile, neutral, or frown)
• Their feelings about us (did we make the cut or not)

Across the top, we listed the schools we would explore, including our current. For most of the schools on the list, we had to schedule visits, do assessments, create essays, and transfer records from our current school. It was a process that, on the best days, was exhausting. But keeping the spirit of exploration and curiosity alive was the only remedy for stagnation. I was willing to keep taking steps, because I knew something needed to shift even though I did not know how or what it was.

STAY TRUE TO THE WHY OF YOUR DESIRE

The hardest part was keeping true to the commitment with the surrounding criticism and naysayers. Extracting yourself from a community who believes, as you had, that the school you're in is the best school for everyone, takes a lot of resilience. I'll never forget a low point when another mother, who I respected, said, "This is the best school for her. I know your daughter, and I know this is it. You would be crazy to move her." That sent me on an emotional swirl.

But here's the crazy thing about walking the innovation journey with an open mind. Life begins to surprise you with unexpected gifts. One day, I told a trusted friend about the process, the details of her diagnosis, and the complexities of the situation. I was wondering aloud how we would make this decision. I told her of an incongruity in the assessments I received from the school versus the new assessments she took during the process. That's when things shifted.

STAY OPEN AS YOU FOLLOW THE YELLOW BRICK ROAD

Although this friend lived in Minnesota, she had had a similar journey with her child. And as her story unfolded, I resonated with what she had to say. Leaving that conversation, I was led to the Gifted Development Center site, which was dedicated to the research and development of the gifted. This led me to another diagnostician. As we followed that trail, a new diagnosis of my daughter emerged: 2E. Twice Exceptional meaning her brain operates on both sides of the Bell Curve of "average." According to the 2E Community of Practice (2E Twice Exceptional Newsletter), 2E students evidence exceptional ability and disability, which results in a unique set of circumstances:

- Their exceptional ability may dominate, hiding their disability.
- Their disability may dominate, hiding their exceptional ability.
- Each may mask the other so that neither is recognized or addressed.

Therefore, 2E students thrive in specialized, enriched education with simultaneous support.

As I continued to read and listen to the diagnostician about the underlying cause, we soon discovered through subsequent testing that a vision processing disorder was creating the other "exception" in her learning. Wow! Understanding her felt like heaven had just revealed a secret. Not only did we have a more specific understanding of the incongruity, but also the behaviors that play out as ADHD.

SOMETIMES THE BEST DECISION IS THE UNEXPECTED ONE

Shortly after learning about this difference, we discovered a tiny private school about thirty miles from where we lived but still within "the circle" of possibility. After her first school visit, she ran into my arms, gushing, telling me about the Valentine's Day beaded black and white bracelet she had made from binary code. I blinked twice, chills spreading. She had visited five private schools and a charter. The reaction was night and day. She continued to tell me eagerly about her other experiences as we drove away and then she became quiet. I glanced in the rearview mirror and saw she was fast asleep. That evening the headmaster called and said, "Often, the first day a student enters our school, they are tired because we are working their brains for the first time in a way they're not accustomed to."

I answered, "She fell asleep in the car on the way home. First time in seven years she's done that."

But this would require a physical move, so definitely a weighted decision.

I didn't know then that we would find a home less than five minutes away from the school. I didn't know that on this property, another desire for my daughter's holistic thriving would be not one but two horses. That these horses would be a part of the emotional therapy she so desperately needed, and the horses' owner would not only take care of the horses and the property while they stayed, but provide lessons for her weekly, during what could possibly be the most transformative year of her life as we navigated the impact of COVID.

USING AN INNOVATION PROCESS BUILT ON EMPATHY MAKES YOU WISER

And, a year later, on her first day of the second year at her new school, I received another quote from her I will keep with me as she grows. "Mom, going to school here is like summer but better. It's so much fun. I love it."

This decision was a wise one, and wisdom appeared as we followed the process. In addition to the life we have built here, her dad now lives only ten minutes away, and they get to spend their weekends together enjoying a plethora of activities we did not even know existed in the area before our move. Using this empathic innovation process changed our lives in ways that were beyond my imagination—beyond what I *knew* was a possibility. The process made me wiser in the same way I had seen my clients over the years become wise in their decision-making.

Wisdom is, according to the New Oxford Dictionary, "the quality of having experience, knowledge, and good judgment." Notice that this definition includes more than just knowledge to be wise. It is knowledge blended with experience.

Empathy allows us to receive a broader perspective. Deciding from this broader perspective makes decision making easier. We become wise in the process. We have integrated knowledge.

FRAMEWORKS SIMPLIFY COMPLEX DECISIONING

But when we start innovating in the unknown, decision-making can seem complex. It is because we are accustomed to making decisions with data, in a binary way. That style works when we have all the data we need.

When innovating with empathy, data is story-driven, emotional. The stories found in the heart, when woven together, create the data we need to decide where to go. It's where we find meaning. But it is hard for our brain to grasp disparate data. It's hard to rationalize or think analytically about unrelated stories.

Frameworks provide a way to break down a complex situation that expands the brain helping us decide with wisdom vs. a typical linear approach.

When searching for my daughter's school, we created a structured "grid" framework to rate each of the criteria across the variety of schools we experimented with.

When we use a model or a framework, we can begin to see the information collected holistically, forcing our perception to change outside of what we could see before.

But sometimes, life forces on us an opportunity to decide without data—in moments we are least expecting it. And for those times, we must use empathy to remember our strengths as a framework to help us decide, even when it hits us unexpectedly.

That is what my friend, Captain Mike, a pilot for a major airline did on a flight he thought would be a normal one.

EMPATHIC DECISIONING REQUIRES US TO LISTEN WITH PRESENCE AND INTENTION

Captain Mike and his co-pilot were in their seats, doing their normal banter prior to take-off. They didn't know each other so the typical small talk consisted of their latest flight experience and the upcoming schedule. For Mike, it was just another day in his more than eighteen-year journey flying for a major airline. Both he and the co-pilot were energized though, because today they were flying into Athens, Greece. Not a bad place to spend a night. He had a faint memory of a peer mentioning: "Don't fly over Sarajevo, Bosnia. Either the US fighter jets will intercept you or you will get shot down."

They had plotted their route into the FMC (Flight Management Computer) which creates their flight plan. So, they were shocked when shortly after take-off, the ATC (air traffic controller) was hot in their ears saying, "We're rerouting you."

Mike looked over and shrugged when his co-pilot asked, "Why are they taking us off the flight plans? Aren't there mountains on this route? We're too low to veer off."

As they veered the plane right, they looked over to the left, and saw why. The sky was unusually cloudy. What looked like a dark storm rose from the earth, sparks shooting up toward the sky. Mike was full of chills as he recognized it was a different kind of storm than he had flown through before. The co-pilot turned again. Their surprise and confusion turned to mutual understanding. They were flying through a war zone.

As if on cue, the ATC said, *"No worries, we'll lead you through it."* This was spoken in a heavy accent neither could recognize. They followed minute-by-minute instructions, not knowing what would come next, completely dependent on a voice they could barely understand. It wasn't long until a new voice activated on the sound system. They learned quickly that they were flying over another country. Still not knowing where they were as they followed a voice with a new accent, listening intently to understand, until a third dispatcher in yet another accent began directing them.

One by one, different dispatchers sounded in their ears as they flew blind through the air, knowing every moment's decision was life-altering. As these trained pilots continued to take direction from the unknown voices from the ground, they were flying blind. They were completely present, simultaneously integrating new information with their internal knowledge.

Mike had flown well over 10,000 hours at this point in his career, which is what most would call an "expert" in any given field.

Not to worry, he thought to himself. *Flying blind is not that difficult because I know what to do.* But as he told me the story, he also explained what he remembered that day about the value of the intense flight training simulation where he built his strengths as a pilot.

DECIDING IS EASIER WHEN YOU ARE PRESENT TO THE BIG PICTURE

For years, these pilots had been given intense simulation experiences. They were designed to throw an immense number of challenges like an engine catching on fire, hydraulic issues, and so on. When a pilot is given enough "taxing" challenges, their brains narrow focus "in the red."

"In the red" means the pilot becomes too focused on one problem. The training helps them learn to stay in the broadest perspective possible, "in the green", so they do not forget to do everything needed to ensure safe flight to landing. One of the things they were trained to do is connect with others to help them through it. That helped them keep their thinking broad.

That day flying over the Bosnian war, Mike realized being forced to connect externally, even without a flight plan, helped him see the bigger picture. It forced the presence to listen intently to their guidance rather than focusing too narrowly "in the red" on "how to solve the problem" as they flew over the war zone.

PRESENCE PUTS US INTO FLOW WHERE WE CAN MAKE INTEGRATED DECISIONS

As I listened to his story, I recognized he was what many call "the flow state." Another way to describe this is being "in the zone," which is the mental state when a person is fully immersed in a feeling of energized focus, full involvement, or complete absorption while doing, resulting in a transformed sense of time.

Flow allows our internal trust to integrate with external information. We become aligned with life where it becomes effortless, internally and with each other. Integrated decision-making in this flow state occurs when the resource, information, and feedback are all aligned in the moment (Kashtan, 2021).

He told me the only way he had a sense of time was due to his constant checking of the fuel level. What he said was profound: "When you're in a state where your body mind and intuition are all connected to do the thing you know how to do, fear is not allowed, you act out of complete creativity." Flow.

It's like an athlete on a field or court who has done the work 10,000 times. A basketball team who intentionally is in "flow" to win a game together operates this way, within the bounds of the court space and time and surrounding energy. They "flow" with intention, being present, aware, instinctive, and creative together.

This is how I feel when leading an interview or discussion. Complete presence, flowing with the information I need, resources I have, and feedback coming toward me. I have been thinking lately about how to live the rest of my life in flow, allowing opportunities to make integrated decisions with more presence with what is rather than resisting what comes at me.

Ultimately, the shifts in our lives can become smaller when we use this approach, instead of bigger. Not because what we want is smaller but because "the next step" will eventually produce "the right step" instead of the other way around. Many in the industry call this a "bias toward action."

Staying present, allowing yourself to flow through the innovation process, being in the unknown, trusting decisions based on integrating them with the information you are receiving, helps you make wise decisions forward—empowered—one small step at a time.

FIRESTARTER SPARKS—EMPATHY HELPS YOU DE-TERMINE WISE DIRECTION FROM HOLISTIC UN-DERSTANDING

1. Decisions Become Clear When You Follow the Process
2. Deciding is Easier When You Begin with Heart-Led Desire
3. Set up Criteria or a Framework for Decision-Making
4. Stay True to the Why of Your Desire
5. Stay Open as You Follow the Yellow Brick Road
6. Sometimes the Best Decision is the Unexpected One
7. Using an Innovation Process Built on Empathy Makes You Wiser
8. Frameworks Simplify Complex Decisioning
9. Empathic Decisioning Requires Us to Listen with Presence and Intention

10. Deciding is Easier When You Are Present to the Big Picture

11. Presence Puts Us into Flow Where We Can Make Integrated Decisions

FIRESTARTER FUEL—IGNITING ME

1. What decisions are you trying to make right now that feel "too hard"? What small action next step could you decide on now?
2. Where is the pressure to decide coming from?
3. Instead of deciding, what could you still learn or discover?
4. Who could help you think about this decision from a broader perspective?
5. How can you look at the data visually in a new way?

FIRESTARTER FUEL—IGNITING WE

1. What are we needing to decide on now?
2. What are the two best options we see as possibility? Where could we find information that could help us create a third option?
3. How do the team members differ in their opinions? What is driving that?
4. What do all members of the team collectively agree on?
5. How could we assess the data by sorting, congregating, separating data so that it brings about new thinking?

PART II

THE BARRIERS TO INNOVATION

Over the years, I have noticed a pattern with my client teams. Regardless of where they are in The Innovation Journey, there are a few common emotional states that individually or collectively keep leaders and teams stuck.

Ironically, as I began to study these more in depth, there is a common theme: there are emotional barriers anchored in anger, fear, or sadness. And while all emotion gives us valuable information, staying in any of these emotional states can block the innovative spirit and keep individuals and teams stagnant and disengaged if we are unaware of the barrier.

Like anything hidden, once exposed, it can be a gift. Barriers are not meant to keep us stuck; they are meant to help us grow. My hope is that as we become aware of these emotional barriers and their impact to problem solving, they will offer a path forward to passionate purpose.

CHAPTER 7

RESISTANCE

It was a hot, dusty, dry summer day in West Texas. I was eleven. Tears spilled down my cheek. I didn't want her to leave. I watched from my grandmother's front kitchen windowsill, perched on the side of the sink. My cousin, just one year younger, walked down the gravel driveway with two suitcases, one in each hand. Head held high, shoulders back, she was confident, unwavering. I couldn't believe she was leaving. My cousin's visits were always the highlight of my summer.

My cousins came every summer from Plano, a suburb of Dallas, Texas. In the eighties, Plano had the high distinction of being the number two "drug capital" high school in the United States, popular for its cocaine abundance. So, my aunt and uncle sent their kids "to the farm" to keep them out of trouble. It was good for them. It was good for all of us!

Our home was next door to my grandparents, only a short walk between the two. But the driveway from the main road to grandmother's house was a good five-minute walk. It was made of caliche rock, and it stirred up dirt as dusty as everything else in West Texas.

There were five of us when my cousins visited, all stair-stepped a year apart. I was the oldest and my brother, the youngest. It was one of our favorite pastimes to fight or compete over who was grandmother's favorite. We all loved her attention. I was the oldest and could brag the loudest about all the reasons I *knew* I was her favorite. Also being the oldest in her family, my cousin fought me over the "favorite" position with our grandmother. It was one of the few things we fought about.

This day, we evidently had ramped up our fighting because in a rare moment, my grandmother suddenly said in a stern voice, "That's enough."

We all stopped, frozen. We almost never heard sternness from her mouth, so it shocked us. My cousin pushed. She wasn't finished fighting yet. And said haughtily, "I know April is your favorite, just admit it!"

My grandmother looked at her and said very calmly, "Yes, in this moment, April is my favorite."

Admittedly, my chest broadened with inner triumph; but externally, my eyes grew wide, and my cheeks grew hot pink. I was mortified my grandmother had let the others in on our secret. I wanted to pull her aside and whisper, "Let's just keep this between us. It will be easier for everyone."

My cousin promptly spun on her ten-year-old heels. She said, shouting backward, "Okay, if that is how you feel, fine. I'm packing my bags and hitchhiking back home!"

I followed, begging her to stay, saying it wasn't true. I resisted her leaving and thought if I could just talk some sense into her, she would forget about the whole thing and stay.

I even gave up my right to being the favorite in my effort to get her to stay. "Please, Grandmother's just kidding. We both know you're her favorite. Everyone does." I made a broad sweep with my arms, pointing to the younger three. My sister rolled her eyes and went back to playing. The two youngest boys never looked up from their Transformers attacking each other.

Grandmother, nonplussed, never looked up, continuing with her household work. "Does no one care?" I shouted out loud. Why was no one worried that our beloved cousin would take off and migrate *by herself* toward home. I couldn't make sense of it.

As my cousin half-packed her disheveled bags in her anger, then made her way through the back door, I grabbed my grandmother's arm. "Grandmother, you have to stop her!"

Grandmother waited until my cousin made her dramatic exit, saw my tears, and asked gently, to herself but with a sparkle in her eyes, *"I wonder how far she will go?"*

Instead of answering, she took my hand and led me to the kitchen and helped me onto the windowsill. We stayed there together, side-by-side, her standing and me sitting perched on the ledge by the sink. We watched my cousin lug bags too heavy for her down the driveway all the way to the end. Still nervous, I looked over at Grandmother, waiting for her to *do* something. And the look on her face showed something I did not recognize at the time. Curiosity, wonder maybe, but there was no resistance.

When she got to the end of the driveway, my cousin stopped. I could not see a lifted thumb but wondered if she was really trying to hitchhike. I don't remember if we watched her for ten minutes or an hour but at some point, my anxiety subsided. It occurred to me that she was never going any farther. Looking back on it, we were in the country. Everyone who traversed the "main road" knew my grandparents. Not one of them would have picked up a child with their thumb up back then except to bring her back down the driveway.

RESISTANCE LIMITS CHOICE, ACCEPTANCE INCREASES FREEDOM TO CHOOSE

My grandmother knew all along exactly how far my cousin would get. She was wondering how long it would take for her to make the choice to turn around. Even though it didn't look like it to me at the time, she had shown great empathy for my cousin. She had allowed her to have her own experience and emotions without trying to control them. She had not resisted my cousin's behavior; she was simply present for it.

Up until then, I experienced my grandmother as the soft, quiet, sparkly-eyed older woman who always had a treat for our eager mouths, whether it was fresh peaches or homemade ice cream with pound cake. After that day, I saw her as a powerful creature, someone who knew something more than most.

My cousin sat down at the end of the driveway. The afternoon whittled away. We got bored of watching her and began playing again. Grandmother continued with her housework. It was close to dusk when my cousin began the walk back toward the house. After setting her suitcase down, she called out to me, "April. Come here. I had an idea." She was excited with her innovative thought. Without mentioning the earlier event, she went on to tell me she had been thinking about a new way we could agree on who would be "Grandmother's favorite."

"How about, we trade days? One of us is grandmother's favorite each day, and then we assign the others their days, too." Joining in her creative thinking, I agreed wholeheartedly, and we went to find paper and pen so we could create a calendar and announce our plan to the rest of the crew.

That day my grandmother taught me something I have never forgotten. Sometimes empathy is just a matter of releasing a grip on controlling someone else's experience— to let it be. Let them be. It is acceptance. She allowed my cousin's reality to be what it was, and in doing so, my cousin was able to experience the fullness of her choice, then make a new empowering one. By accepting her feelings as they were, without resisting them, she created freedom to choose—real choice instead of controlled choice.

One of the biggest barriers to innovation is resistance to what is. By accepting what is through the lens of empathy, real innovation can begin because it increases the choices available to us.

FREEDOM TO CHOOSE EXPANDS OUR THINKING AND ABILITY TO INNOVATE

This kind of empathy—the acceptance of what is, of another's reality—helps us better direct our creations. It takes us out of spinning trying to create something others don't want or create something for the wrong people. Releasing our "grip" on something that will not change helps expand our thinking.

Freedom comes from releasing our "grip" on things like:

1. Who we think people "should" be
2. What other people "should" believe
3. How they "should" behave
4. How they "should" feel

Everything we believe "should be" keeps us trapped in an unproductive thinking habit because we are focused on changing something that, ultimately, is not our choice to change. But when we accept things, people, and situations as they are, our thinking expands. When our thinking expands, new thoughts and possibilities enter our realm.

It opens us up to new and different experiences which enhances innovation.

RESISTANCE KEEPS US STUCK, ACCEPTANCE HELPS US CREATE WITH REALITY

As long as we are stuck in a spiral of wanting to change someone or something that cannot be changed, we will block our ability to create what we deeply desire. Sometimes we resist what others want or don't want. Instead of accepting their desire, we push to create for them, and it leaves us in a spiral of confusion when what we offer does not align.

The truth is, we really can't change what others do. Often we can't change our specific situation, and in that moment, the faster we accept the reality of what is ours to change and what is not, is the moment we rise above circumstance and begin creating more of what we want. Our abilities are strengthened because we create with reality, instead of against it.

Sometimes we resist what we want. When we dishonor our own desires and refuse to place boundaries around us and lines in the sand, when we show up for anyone and anything, it minimizes our ability to create. Shapeshifting is not the way of an empowered innovator. That is called people-pleasing. People-pleasing is the opposite of what good marketers do.

Resisting "what is" can keep us whirling in motion like dust in a storm, yet still not moving forward. This leaves us lonely, angry, and frustrated. These feelings are "sandbags," holding us down, blocking us from creativity, and moving our ideas into action.

But when we let go of blame and shame, and return to desire with empathy, we can expand and make a mental shift. Desire grounds us in the truth of what we value. And our truth-led values can lead us to new discovery and, ultimately, better creations.

ACCEPTING REALITY CREATES CLARITY AND STRENGTHENS YOUR INNOVATION

One of my many brilliant clients created clarity out of confusion by releasing resistance to what consumers understood, and instead accepted and worked with the reality of their target segment.

It was our fifth focus group. As I walked from the front room where I had been talking for the past hour to a group of six consumers, to the back room where my clients were listening, I stopped to take a breath. I assumed they would be buzzing with conversation. As I entered, there was silence. I sensed the tension. They were exasperated.

One of the developers, a brilliant leader and product scientist in his mid-forties, said, "I don't understand why they're not getting it. They say they don't want an 'orangey-looking tan,' they say they don't like using sunless tanners because it looks 'fake,' and here we are giving them a product that will not only help them achieve the proper color based on their skin's undertone, but it will also look more natural. Why are they saying they don't want it?"

Another woman, early thirties, marketer, piped up: "They want it. They just don't understand it. We haven't found the right language."

Then the insights leader added, "And the bigger problem is, they don't even know the language for how to describe their skin's undertone. So, without a common knowledge of language, we're going to keep confusing them by explaining how it works."

When teams get in this predicament, it's challenging. Their desire is to not only create a product that solves the problem but to ensure it is communicated in a way consumers desire. They must emotionally connect with the problem to solve and then provide a benefit that is emotionally rewarding.

This product had been two years in the making, they were under a deadline to bring it to market, and here they were: stuck. They had already conducted significant research, enough to know that most people don't really understand what their skin's undertone is. This was their third attempt to bring the product line to life, and still, they could sense it would be hard to pass the next stage in the product development process with what they were hearing, yet again. Their communication efforts to help people understand the product were meager at best.

RELEASING CONTROL OF OTHERS' PERCEPTIONS ALLOWS US TO EXPAND OURS

Then, something interesting happened. A question from someone I had not heard from throughout the research was posed. He was new, quiet, on the product development team, and in his late twenties. He had come recently from a toy company with a different culture. He was accustomed to churning out more toy products every quarter than most companies do in two years. He said: "Okay, so what if we can't educate them on the language? What if it's not the right time for the whole product line. Then what would we do?"

When I hear questions like "what if...?" and "then what...?" my eyes smile, and my heart does a little dance. What he did was stop resisting what consumers knew about their skin's undertone. Instead, he offered acceptance into a room that had been resistant to a very clear fact. And when he did that, everyone's thinking expanded. They began talking about what they already knew. They already knew that their product could "darken the skin" regardless of the undertone.

And then the research shifted. Instead of fighting the reality and continuing to "educate" the market on the product(s) they were trying to bring into the market, they decided to learn what consumers *do* know about their skin's undertone, if anything. Once we shifted the line of questioning, the team eventually changed the communication so that it hit home in a compelling way. Instead of creating confusion at the shelf like many of their competitors were doing, they created compelling communication tied directly to how consumers viewed their skin's undertone. Keywords and messaging could be put together in a way that was clear and, therefore, resulted in a purchase.

And while theirs was not the first product to customize shade based on skin undertone, their line became an immediate hit in the market. Their first-year sales were grossly underestimated. They could not keep product on the shelf.

When we release what we cannot control, it helps us expand what we think about, creating room for us to narrow in on what we are meant to create. When we stop trying to convince others of our point of view and instead lean in to understand what is most important to bring our creation to life and accept a new point of view as a way to expand our own, it gives us a bigger and better playing ground in which to create.

FIRESTARTER SPARKS—EMPATHY TRANSFORMS RESISTANCE TO ACCEPTANCE

1. Resistance Limits Choice, Acceptance Increases Freedom to Choose
2. Freedom to Choose Expands Our Thinking and Ability to Innovate
3. Resistance Keeps Us Stuck, Acceptance Helps Us Create with Reality
4. Accepting Reality Creates Clarity and Strengthens Your Innovation

5. Releasing Control of Others' Perceptions Allows Us to Expand Ours

FIRESTARTER FUEL—IGNITING ME
1. What is one thing that seems to be limiting your freedom or choice—something out of your control to change?
2. What if you could never change that, what would you do then?
3. What else could be a possibility if you shifted either who or what you were focused on changing?
4. What is one shift you have complete control over in this circumstance? What is another possibility? Or a third that you could completely control if you allowed other things or people to be who or what they are?

FIRESTARTER FUEL—IGNITING WE
1. What is something that seems to be "unchangeable" on your team, project, or organization?
2. What is one thing you struggle with accepting about the team or organization you're in/leading/supporting?
3. What if the thing you're holding onto or resisting about your team is not about you but about something bigger, what would you do, think, or say next?
4. What could be shifted or possibly created even with these circumstances?
5. What would open up if you welcomed the unchangeable circumstance or person as it is?

CHAPTER 8

PERFECTION

Our interview was a little more than halfway over when Alice said something that shocked me.

Alice was an executive leader for a large automotive corporation. Some would call her a "rock star." She had risen to the top easily. Her business acumen was well-rounded. She was a brilliant, bold, and beautiful leader, internally and externally. Her technical strength in finance and compassionate, thoughtful communication skills earned her the respect and admiration of her peers, leaders, and especially the teams who reported to her. I had been captivated by her vulnerability and grateful for her willingness to participate in the study. Throughout the interview she increasingly became more open with me about the why of her "passion" project.

This interview was a result of my own "passion" project. For the first time in my career, I decided to innovate by conducting a research study I was passionate about: the themes and patterns of "empathy in innovation." I was curious to understand the struggles and challenges of personal innovation versus the organizational innovation I was accustomed to.

Even though I was talking to her through my computer via Zoom, I could sense her compassion and strength. Her bright blue eyes could light up a room, her positivity is contagious.

That's why I was surprised to see tears fill her eyes suddenly when I asked, "What do you think you struggle with the most in your creative endeavor?"

Her answer was simple, one word. "*Perfectionism.*" I was shocked at the vulnerability along with the emotional reaction it evoked for her. As soon as she said it, her eyes welled up. It softened me, as I recognized the role perfectionism had in my own life. I knew the struggle was real and immediately sensed that, in many ways, this tendency was why she was great in her career. As I listened, I realized what it cost her.

PERFECTIONISM PREVENTS US FROM OUR MOST IMPACTFUL WORK

As she wiped a tear away, she said, "What if I could learn to say to those I lead, whether it's my family or my team, 'I don't always know what I'm doing either.' You know what I think it would do for them? It would allow the others around me to relax enough, to exhale while they're getting the work done."

On the outside, her life looks sublime: she has a wonderful career. Year after year, opportunities had been handed to her as she climbed the corporate ladder. She has three amazing kids, all doing well in school. She was backed by a husband who supported her career and acted as a partner, providing both financially with his career along with support with home management.

Her creative project was: Becoming Me: 2.0.

When we began the interview, I asked her to expand on why she chose *"Becoming Me: 2.0" as her creative endeavor. She answered, "I reached a point not too long ago that I realized my mental CPU would burn out if I didn't stop multitasking so much. I need to create Becoming Me: 2.0 because while multitasking is how I've survived this whole time, I'm missing out on what's happening in the present most of the time."*

"Tell me more," I encouraged. "What is the relationship between perfectionism and multi-tasking?"

She went on to say the recurring pattern she was seeing in her life is the endless to-do list of "easy to fix" solutions. These were what kept her occupied. In fact, they kept her going, giving her an adrenaline hit every time she checked off something easy.

She said, *"I'm great at my job because of my ability to multitask. I know exactly what to do to move the needle forward, to perform, and help others perform. It's so easy to keep doing*

what I'm great at. I get a quick hit, it's easier to focus on the
quick hits than a bigger problem that doesn't feel solvable."

PERFECTIONISM DECREASES LEADERSHIP EFFECTIVENESS

She went on: "I'm starting to realize many of us as leaders have a ton of fear and anxiety. We don't feel we are good enough; we're striving to perfect, to achieve. Very rarely do I see leaders acknowledge our own fears, and I believe that puts pressure on everyone below you. People below you in an organization start to internalize the fear we at the top are feeling.

But the need to be perfect keeps me stuck with my project for two reasons:

1. It causes me to procrastinate on my most important items.
2. When I make a mistake, I tend to ruminate.

Both lessen my effectiveness as a leader."

I was amazed, not only at her self-awareness but her openness about it. I challenged her about her self-reflections. "It seems to me you are very open about this awareness, at least that's what I see."

Again, her response was profound: "The more I admit how much I struggle with this, the easier it is for me to do something about it. Just telling you is therapeutic. In fact, it made me think of someone with whom I have not been as transparent as I can be. And I just made a note to fix it."

Wow, I thought. *What a concept.* I wondered where she had learned this. I don't remember any curriculum in my Executive MBA program addressing executive transparency. As far as I could tell, most executives had not learned this in their formal training, either. But first, I had a question about her above two points.

"Can you give me an example of the type of things you are avoiding doing in your quest of Becoming Me: 2.0, because they're difficult to perfect?"

CHOOSING PRESENCE OVER PERFECTIONISM CREATES POSSIBILITY

At first she hesitated, then, with a deep exhale and a shift slowing her rhythm and lowering her tone, she said, "Okay, I'll tell you a story of what happened last night where my perfectionism caused me to procrastinate and ruminate on my failure."

She began describing, with regret, what had happened in her kitchen the night before. She was pulling out dinner for the family. Even though her body was gathering plates and assembling the quick fix supper, her mind was not there. "I was back in my four o'clock meeting, replaying the dynamics in my mind. I was responsible for leading my peers through a decision we needed to agree on for the CEO. It did not go as planned." She said two of her peers had a debate that quickly turned into an argument. Twenty minutes later, the whole room became so heated they decided to adjourn without reaching an agreement.

"While I was physically preparing dinner to get on the table, I mentally was in the middle of that meeting and ready to get back to my computer so I could fire off a couple of emails. The thought of 'fixing it' had me mentally preoccupied with developing a strategy. That's when one of the kids came in and asked a question. I turned around and with exasperation, said sharply, 'What is it?' Then, I went on to tell them all sternly to stay out of the kitchen so I could finish."

Her expression shifted as she said with regret, "That's when I looked at my little five-year-old's eyes and felt simultaneous guilt, shame, and frustration. I became aware I would rather write the email than fix his hurt because it was easier to do that. I knew how to write the email, but I did not know how to fix the sad face I had created by my reaction to his innocent question."

She continued intently, "I get a lot of self-esteem from problem-solving and small successes, and that's not what parenting gives you. Parenting is not a sprint, it's a marathon. I notice I get frantic. If I'm not in constant motion to figure out the next thing, then I feel like I'm going to get further behind."

Alice told me that after she became aware of the impact of snapping at her son, she made a sudden choice. She left the plates of lukewarm food untouched in the kitchen and stopped her internal mental chatter. Instead, she went to the living room and sat down on the floor without saying a word.

As we spoke, she smiled and wiped away another tear. But this time, it was one of joy as she allowed the memory in of her sweet son climbing in her lap so he could proudly show her the Lego blocks he had just put together. That decision delayed dinner by only about five minutes, but it gave her rich progress toward her passion project goal: becoming more present.

This event also helped her see that a few minutes of presence saved time versus the amount of time she had spent spiraling, rethinking the meeting. She said, "Not only did I realize it was stopping me from my goal of Becoming Me: 2.0, it was lessening my productivity in general. When you re-analyze every word you said in a meeting, the bad feelings can create an undercurrent of stagnation. It's not fun to be in that spiral."

As she described her story and I witnessed the emotional challenge she was describing, it struck me as ironic. By choosing to connect with her son, to just "be with" the damage she felt she had created by snapping at him rather than creating a plan or strategizing how to do "damage control," she simultaneously reduced the "downward spiral" of regret from her earlier meeting.

By connecting in the moment with her son just where he was, she was able to move out of her rumination and into presence, thus new possibilities with her son.

She might not have realized the extent of it, but I could see Alice was on her way to Becoming Me: 2.0, little by little. She was finding small ways to move from "checking things off," letting go of perfection, and allowing herself to be present in simple connection.

Alex Korb, neuroscientist and author of *The Upward Spiral* talks about one way to reverse the course of depression, one small change at a time is to: "Go for good enough. Worrying is often triggered by wanting to make the perfect choice or by trying to maximize everything. [...] If you try to have the best of everything, you're likely to be paralyzed by indecision or dissatisfied with your choice. In fact, this kind of 'maximizing' has been proven to increase depression. So don't try to make the most amazing dinner; start out by just making a good dinner. Don't try to be the perfect parent; just be a good one. Don't try to be your happiest; just be happy."

That's what great innovators do. They step through the messy process of the hard unknown by allowing imperfection to exist.

The best innovators are ones who know that perfection is the enemy of innovation. If we can see the innovation process as a system for learning and creating, it helps us move through the stages with more peace as we connect instead of perfect.

PERFECTIONISM CREATES RUMINATION AND DISCONNECTION

Rumination is the mental habit of overthinking a past event. Examples include focusing on past mistakes, another's offense toward you, or flaws and weaknesses. And while it may be a hard pill to swallow, repetitive negative thoughts are a part of being human.

Psychotherapist Scott Kohner in his blog article, *The Ugly Side of Perfectionism and Rumination*, writes about the relationship between perfectionism and rumination, saying: "Perfectionists are prone to rumination, and rumination is one symptom of both depression and anxiety. In short, when you ruminate, you replay negative experiences or thoughts in your head repeatedly. For perfectionists, that can take the form of focusing on a perceived failure or a time when they fell short of the mark. They feel imperfect and inadequate, and rumination reinforces that unhealthy view of themselves."

However, that doesn't mean hope is lost. As seen in Alice's story above, empathic connection allows your neuropathways to begin firing in a different region.

In the end, perfection is just a concept—an impossibility we use to torture ourselves and that contradicts nature. Studies including one published in *Journal of Research in Personality*, according to an article by Eric W. Dolan of PsyPost "indicate that perfectionism leads to depressive symptoms, by generating stress and social disconnection. Greater perfectionistic concerns were associated with heightened stress and social disconnection, while greater perfectionistic strivings were associated with heightened social disconnection but not stress.

The findings indicate that 'people high in perfectionistic concerns appear to think, feel, and behave in ways that increase the likelihood of experiencing and eliciting stressful events, leaving them vulnerable to depressive symptoms,' the researchers explained.

In addition, 'establishing meaningful connections with others is often difficult for people high in perfectionistic concerns, as others' approval, acceptance, and love are judged as forthcoming only if they achieve perfect outcomes. Likewise, people high in perfectionistic strivings frequently pursue agentic goals, at the expense of collective goals, which we speculate causes them to miss or ignore chances for participating in meaningful relationships, which, in turn, leads to depressive symptoms.'

CHOOSING EMPATHIC CONNECTION OVER PERFECTION ENHANCES OUR CREATIONS

The way to break the pattern of our human tendency is through empathic discovery. It creates a break in the loop when we question our thinking with empathy.

Authentic connection can move us from perfectionism to greater productivity. When people come together to work on a problem for a common purpose, an exponential number of connections can be made. It not only relieves stress for the creator but also creates endorphins and oxytocin which combat depression.

Our tendency to perfect before connecting can begin when we are young, and the systems we live in that reward perfection exacerbate the problem. Witnessing the power of connection to heal the need to perfect makes an impact.

I recently saw this play out when my daughter became upset. She was beside herself, almost in a panic. Her breathing was ragged and sharp—big gestures, as she shut her computer down hard. "I can't do it, Mom," she cried.

I looked up, and asked, "What can you not do?"

"I'm supposed to meet for my group project on Zoom in fifteen minutes, but I can't meet with them because I did not finish my part," she said, her voice rising to let me know how stressed she was.

"Well, why can't you do it?" I was still not sure why this was so urgent.

"I can't figure it out," she cried loudly as if I were deaf and could not understand her language.

"Do you want me to help you, or why don't you just jump on and let them know where you're stuck?" I thought it was an obvious answer. I then realized what I had been missing as she literally started crying, sobbing.

"Mom, I don't understand how to do it. They're expecting me to do my part. I cannot show up without doing my part. They will all be so maaaad at me."

What was becoming clear was her need to be perfect before connecting. *How many times have I done the same?* I asked myself. How often did I show up not doing at least a hundred percent of what I had agreed to do? It was exhausting. I attempted to soothe her verbally, even reason with her, but it was not to be. So, instead, I sat next to her, stroking her back, remembering how many times I had felt this. I then put my arm around her ten-year-old shoulders. And we rocked back and forth to the music playing.

I noticed the time, knowing her Zoom meeting was about to start. I said, "Well, I need to do a few things in the other room. Your choice is to stay in here and figure it out alone or reach out and see what happens." I walked out but had all my attention directed toward her from the adjacent living room; I heard her breathing, this time, slow, deep breaths. She took three of them. Then, what happened next was astounding.

I watched this child, who was panicked a few minutes before, lead the Zoom conversation with courageous vulnerability. "Hey guys, I have a little bit of a problem. I can't figure out how to do one of the things on my list."

One of the other girls chimed in and said, "Share your screen, let's see what it is." My daughter did. I was closer now, watching her on the couch from the kitchen while I was doing the dishes. The next thing I knew, the entire group of four, my daughter included, "hovered and work-shopped" the challenge. What amazed me was not only how the group connected, working together to help her figure out a solution to the problem, but they became even more creative because of it.

CHOOSING CONNECTION OVER PERFECTION BUILDS COURAGE

It also provided an amazing learning opportunity—for me and her—to see the power of connecting with courage, to say the thing you do not want to say, and to connect with showing up as less-than-perfect. Courage is built when innovating through the willingness to leave perfection at the door and walk through it with vulnerability instead. When we connect with empathy to ourselves, then others, we move from fear-based thinking to creative thinking.

Perfectionism can put us in a cage. As long as we are perfecting and performing to prove and please, we disallow the contribution and the collaboration of others. You try, try, try to do it alone when perfection becomes the driving force. You feel that to connect with others, you must get it right. But it is the reverse order of things. You need help from others before you can get it right. When you connect in your vulnerability with others, suddenly you can perfect what it is you're trying to achieve, while building your courage bank!

FIRESTARTER SPARKS—EMPATHY TRANSFORMS PERFECTION TO CONNECTION

1. Perfectionism Prevents Us from Our Most Impactful Work
2. Perfectionism Decreases Leadership Effectiveness

3. Choosing Presence Over Perfection Creates Possibility
4. Perfectionism Creates Rumination and Disconnection
5. Choosing Empathic Connection Over Perfection Enhances Our Creations
6. Choosing Connection Over Perfection Builds Courage

FIRESTARTER FUEL—IGNITING ME

1. What is one thing you're procrastinating on, something that feels too big for the time you have to do it?
2. Who could be a good sounding board or accountability partner to help you think about it?
3. What is one conversation you have had that you could think about with a new perspective?
4. What areas do you not worry about or feel the need to be perfect? Why?
5. How can you transfer that thinking to the areas where you worry or care more about perfection?

FIRESTARTER FUEL—IGNITING WE

1. How is the team set up to win "with" each other now?
2. In what areas do you feel like you need to be perfect with your team?
3. What would happen if each member of your team was able to come to a meeting with a problem they are having instead of a solution?
4. What would happen if the team was taught to help each other with their challenging work?
5. How could creativity be instilled in a team by allowing them each a way to show courageous vulnerability?

CHAPTER 9

CONFUSION

"This is definitely not what I was expecting!" I said to Claire as we stood side by side in the onion field. We were hoeing weeds in a small town just north of Amsterdam in the Netherlands. We were twenty-two and had landed from the States just a few hours prior. We would be here six months, staying with six different families during our cultural exchange program with a "free to roam" month built in. But here I was—confused, jet-lagged, and heated both emotionally and physically.

"What in the world?" she replied. "I don't understand why your host dad put us straight to work in the field. I'm hungry and think I might be sick. I can't wait until my host family picks me up. Oh wait, what if I have to hoe weeds in their field, too?"

As her attention drifted away, contemplating what else might be in store for her, my stomach grumbled. I was hungry too. It had been a more than eleven-hour flight from my home in Lubbock, Texas, not including the ride from the airport. It had been a silent ride. Claire and I were both tired. Tired enough to nod off. I rested my head on the back window after I realized my host dad had so little to say.

When I got off the plane, I had been thrilled and a little overwhelmed with the sheer number of people, bikes, and noises as I exited the airport. I knew to hold tightly to my bag given the imminent theft in the city. But I wasn't scared. I was ready. I had so much discovery to do. Everything was new and waiting for me. It would be amazing, I just knew it. I was eager to learn what I didn't know. But I could have never guessed what my reality would be. Yes, there would be much to learn...

Once I found Claire, we ventured down the sidewalk together, leaving the safety of the airport into the unknown city, filled with the tallest people I had ever seen and what felt like orderly mayhem. We were to look for a sign with my name on it—my first of six host families would pick us up and take us both to their home. Claire's family would pick her up from there.

It took a lot of hard work and coordination to find funding and resources for my exchange trip, and my parents were worried about me traveling so far away. However, with some effort, I was able to work everything out and was so excited to start the journey.

Even with a father who was reluctant to send me overseas and a boyfriend who was equally nervous about the unknown of what the next six months would entail, I made a commitment to myself that this was what I was meant to do. I assured the people I loved in my life that I

would be careful and that they would be in my heart, as
I hugged them goodbye. I never questioned the decision.
It was extremely clear. There was no confusion.

CONFUSION IS INEVITABLE IN THE INNOVATION JOURNEY, REGARDLESS OF WHEN IT OCCURS

When we found my host father just outside the airport,
he did not make eye contact. He grabbed one of my
bags out of my hand quickly, spun back around, and
began walking. Claire and I looked at each other confused, shrugged, then followed. We walked in silence
to his car, which was parked in a remote, flat parking
area a few blocks from the airport. In silence, we got
into the car, and in silence we proceeded to drive outside the city and into the flat farmland sprawling in
all directions.

At first, the silence did not bother me. There was so much
new to see. Everything was different: the roundabouts,
the signs, the bikers we had to swerve to miss, the coffee shops, and the people. They looked different: their
chic clothes, their height. They were beautiful, they wore
scarves, and they had bags and shoes I had never seen
before. I noticed everything that was different.

As the beautiful green farmland gently enveloped us,
surrounding us in every direction, I turned toward my
host father, hoping to say something clever and landing
on, "Wow—the Netherlands is just as flat as it is in West
Texas!"

Nothing.

Maybe he didn't hear me, I thought. I looked back at Claire and she shrugged. She had heard me.

I tried again. "I've never seen so many bikes. I'm glad we're not going to your home in one."

No response. *Wow,* I thought. *He must be shy.*

About twenty minutes later he looked over at me and then he started talking to me in fast Dutch. I swirled around, begging for Claire's help silently. Again, she shrugged.

They told me I was going to a country where everyone spoke English, I thought. I had prepped as much as I could on my Dutch, but I was so grateful to go where languages were their strong suit because they were not mine.

When he noticed I didn't understand a word he was saying he finally said in extremely choppy English, "You hungry?"

Grateful, I said, "Yes! I am."

It was three in the afternoon when we pulled in, and I was starving. As we drove up the road to the red thatch Dutch farm home, I noticed the large, beautiful windmill just behind it. Their luscious fields, I discovered later, were all organic. It was something you would see in National Geographic—beautiful, perfect.

His wife, Caroline met us at the door, looking us both up and down with a sharp eye. She wasn't any more excited to see us than he had been but was definitely more interested. She pointed to the table where she had left some coffee and two biscuits before marching back into the house. I sat there waiting for more interaction.

Again, not the welcome I had expected. As soon as we finished our last bite of the cookie biscuit, the host father came around the corner with two hoes in his hand. I watched, expecting him to pass us by to deliver them to someone who helped him on the farm. I did not realize that was me—yours truly. After much back-and-forth with the translation, and complete confusion for both myself and Claire, our bafflement increased because we were given an immediate assignment we could have never expected: we were to use the hoes to chop weeds out of his onion field.

With the same clothes we had traveled in, bags on the porch unpacked, still hungry and exhausted from the trip, we went into the field and began this physical activity of looking for, finding, and chopping weeds out of the host family's onion field.

CONFUSION KEEPS US STUCK BECAUSE THE VOICES IN OUR HEAD TAKE OVER OUR THINKING

And that's where the confusion set in.

What in the world is happening? said one voice in my head.

Another voice argued, *it's going to be fine. Maybe this is a cultural norm or test.*

Yes, the voice convinced me, *we will all laugh at the joke they had on my behalf, and he will slap me on the back saying I have passed with flying colors. Yes, that must be it.*

That got me through another thirty minutes before I collapsed. I literally fell, then sat down on the damp ground. I was so tired from the trip and the confusion.

"That's it," I said out loud to Claire. "I'm going in." She looked at me in gratitude and followed me.

But there was no laughter when I returned to the house. Silence again. It was only a few minutes before Claire's host family came to get her. We hugged, both wondering what in the world we had just embarked on.

Although the meal later was delicious, fresh and healthy—homemade breads, spreads, meats, butters, and even chocolate sprinkles—the lack of conversation at the table was awkward and further puzzled me. *Did I do something wrong? Are they already mad at me?*

After brief gestures directing me toward my bedroom with a note to "be ready by 8:00 a.m.," I was gifted with an alarm clock, made my way to my room, and—without changing my clothes—fell into bed.

Even through my heavy exhaustion, I laid with eyes wide, trying to breathe deeply but confusion laced with anxiety crept in. The back-and-forth continued. *What have I gotten myself into?* versus *It'll be better tomorrow. Yes. You can do anything for three weeks, April—anything.*

The next morning, I was given a chore list, starting with washing floor-to-ceiling windows occupying every wall in the home. I was greeted shortly after breakfast with a ladder, a squeegee, and a bucket of water. The task took most of that day, as I had never washed windows before and my first attempt was not good enough. I was asked to do it again.

A couple of days later after doing most of the household work, I was presented with a list for the bathroom cleaning. In very broken English, my host mom informed me she was going to the hair salon and I needed to have the bathroom cleaned before she returned. I did it. But upon her inspection, I was asked to do it again.

Looking back now, it still surprises me that I remained in this confused state not understanding the situation, even for a week, let alone three. But sometimes when our brains are given too much information to process at once, it is challenging to make sense of everything. In addition to these unusual circumstances with the host family, my boyfriend in the States had lost his dad and I found myself answering his grieving calls. It was easier to process his situation than my own.

CONFUSION IS A RESULT OF INCONGRUENT EXPECTATIONS AND NEW PERCEPTIONS

And so life went on like this for about eight days. A little over a week after we arrived, the country coordinator of the program gathered us so we could all meet each other. There were five of us from the States living with different Dutch families. She had us come for a full day of activity, including a Dutch festival, cheese making tour, and outdoor picnic on the cheese farm.

I remained stoic for most of the day. I had committed to brevity and determination to see it through. But story after story of the others' experiences started to soften what was lurking below the surface of my own emotions. I heard of the adventures they were having, stories of the generosity of their host families, who they had connected with, and what they had learned. Their experiences were so vastly different than mine that the confusion in my mind increased.

AUTHENTIC CONNECTIONS REDUCE CONFUSION AND MOVE US FORWARD

Eventually the conversation turned toward me when someone asked excitedly, "So, April, how has your experience been?" I looked at Claire, who knew, and my eyes brimmed over. And like that, I burst into tears. I did not think I had words for my experience but in that moment, I had a growing self-awareness that no matter how I justified the situation or their behavior, or how much I blamed myself for getting into it, I was not getting what I needed.

I needed the social, emotional, and intellectual connections I had come here to learn.

And because I was in safe company and they were willing to wait for my tears to subside, I eventually told the story of my lack of connection or the experience I yearned for since I had been in Holland.

The program coordinator, who was just a little older than us, was outraged as she listened. At first, she wanted to pull me from the family immediately, the same day. But after a couple of calls to others administering the program, it was decided they would meet with my host parents to better understand what was happening from their perspective.

The next day, my host father asked or rather motioned me to take a drive to meet up with the country coordinator. And, since I was getting good at sign language, I followed their exchange. Although the conversation between them was in Dutch, it became clear there was a misunderstanding about the program goals.

My hosts believed I was in a farm work program where, in exchange for room and board, I would conduct farm labor chores. They were unhappy with me, too, because I was, as it turns now, "not a very good farmworker." (I was a little indignant at this sentiment given I had grown up on a farm, but I let it go). Turns out, the reason they put me on strict household cleaning duty was to "make up for my lack of farm skills."

So, with the misunderstanding out of the way, I was given a choice. I could stay with a promise that things at the house would shift to give me the opportunities aligned with the program: cultural and community connection. Or I could transfer to another home.

I decided to stick it out for the remaining ten days. I had committed to making it work, and my pride wanted to see it through. It was a little strained, but things shifted slightly—no more bathroom cleaning at least.

Eventually the three weeks were up. I went to live with five additional host families, and they were all amazing, lovely, and spoke English as well as I did. I found discoveries made beyond what I could imagine and formed a love for the country and its people. I keep up with some of my families today. It was a foundational experience for me.

The lesson I learned was mostly about how to move from confusion to clarity. Confusion occurs when our current reality does not match up with our expectations. And I learned that when I addressed the confusing issues with authenticity, it was easier to move through to the other side.

UNDERSTANDING EMOTIONAL NEEDS REDUCES CONFUSION

Later, toward the end of the program when I got together with the host coordinator, she said something very profound: "April, my job is to protect the integrity of the program and that means I have to know what's going on with those who are staying with the families. I need to know what you need in order to provide in the way that this program is meant to. It is your job to understand what you need so that you get it."

I couldn't identify what I needed when I was in judgment. Judgment kept me in confusion. When I vacillated between judging myself, making myself feel wrong for not better preparing, and then judging my host family, I stayed stuck and disempowered. The question I asked myself for days was disempowering. *How could this host family believe I was there to be an unpaid laborer?*

But when I left that aside, and instead, connected with myself in an honest way and expressed it to someone who I thought could help, I was able to move out of my confusion.

Confusion, just like anger, can be a gift if we pause and see it for what it is—a mask for fear. Confusion is a gift because it allows us to pause to make sense of our surroundings. But if we stay stuck in confusion, it can become a downward spiral leading to loneliness, isolation, and eventually anger built on blaming and shaming.

From a neuroscience perspective, our brain seeks ways to correlate data and make sense of it. Until it does, it will "stay confused" because confusion is a mask for fear.

When you are confused about direction, it is because fear is creating a "pause" for you. It is waiting for you to move from judgment to empathy.

EMPATHY MIGRATES US FROM CONFUSION TO CLARITY

When we use empathy to uncover what is going on emotionally and use it to our advantage, we can see it for the gift it is—an opportunity to become aware.

My clients are masters at moving from confusion to clarity by using empathy. Here's one example of how clarity arises when you seek to understand.

I had an innovation team who had a cult following—they created indulgent cakes sold in their own retail stores. The team wanted to create "sample size" limited-time offers (LTOs) they could rotate to drive sales but also wanted to ensure these LTOs would resonate with their loyal users. So, we went out to better understand what their loyal customers thought about their mini-sized LTO ideas. They were shocked to learn users were not happy about them at all. These loyal customers did not want to be interrupted from what they expected from the brand. Instead of increasing loyalty with their core customer base, it confused them.

The small cakes they offered were not only too far away from their loyal customer's habit of buying cakes for a group gathering but also the new flavors were too far outside their comfort level. The team was baffled. How could they continue to innovate and drive sales for new customers yet keep their loyal customers on board? They needed to expand on their foundation.

After capturing the confusing learnings and discerning the biggest themes of our surprising findings, they reframed the problem with a simple question. "What can we offer for a limited time that aligns with our loyal consumer's strongest habits?" With the empathic reframe, we went back to discover in-depth about their habits and why they were important. That eventually led to a hybrid solution to create classics with a twist and communicate about the habitual rituals in their marketing. They were able to create a story around their LTOs that emotionally resonated, which drove new sales with their loyal users and pulled new customers into the category.

CONFUSION HELPS US BRIDGE THE GAP BETWEEN WHAT WE KNOW AND NEED TO KNOW

Often confusion helps us see the duality of life: that two things can exist simultaneously. Confusion arises when we are up against something our brain refuses to process and yet it is hitting us in the face to "figure it out." We can often feel frustrated in our confusion, but if we let it, is a gift because it forces our brains to slow down and be guided so that we can make the best choice available.

The best way our brains can process something big is to break it down into the smallest components. Whether it's trying to figure out how to put together IKEA furniture, aligning with an engineer when you're not one, or stopping a whirl of internal confusion over whether to ask for a promotion or not, we can get paralyzed in decisions because we do not want to make the "wrong" one.

Empathy activates our wisdom because it gives our brain a break. When we empathize we activate the heart. That activation gives us confidence to take a small step forward to see what happens. It helps us break things down again into something manageable. It lets us solve the puzzle of confusion we face by putting the edge pieces on first.

FIRESTARTER SPARKS—EMPATHY TRANSFORMS CONFUSION TO CONFIDENCE

1. Confusion is Inevitable in the Innovation Journey, Regardless of When It Occurs
2. Confusion Keeps Us Stuck Because the Voices in Our Head Take Over Our Thinking
3. Confusion is a Result of Incongruent Expectations and New Perceptions
4. Authentic Connections Reduce Confusion and Move Us Forward
5. Understanding Emotional Needs Reduces Confusion
6. Empathy Migrates Us from Confusion to Clarity
7. Confusion Helps Us Bridge the Gap Between What We Know and Need to Know

FIRESTARTER FUEL—IGNITING ME

1. What are you confused about in this situation?
2. What is already clear to you about this situation?
3. In what ways can you break down the information I see in a more manageable way?
4. Who could help shine light on this situation?
5. What has happened in the past that feels similar?

FIRESTARTER FUEL—IGNITING WE

1. What are we collectively confused about?
2. How do others outside of our core team see this situation and why?
3. What is underneath the confusion? What could happen if we chose a path and moved forward? What is another path? And a third?
4. How can we categorize or compartmentalize the information we need in a new way?
5. If we reframed the problem to solve, what would we need to learn to move from confusion to clarity?

CHAPTER 10

LONELINESS

I was sitting alone one night at the fairly new neighborhood Mexican joint that my ex and I used to frequent often. It was a popular place. This wasn't the first time I had ventured out alone. In fact, over the last couple of years, I appreciated being able to take time to travel solo, exploring new things when my daughter was with her dad. While I had friends I could travel with, it was challenging to coordinate with other moms who did not have the freedom to pick up and go on my schedule. In many ways, it was restorative to spend time in my own thoughts and feelings after so many years of spending all my time with others' feelings—both professionally and personally. I experienced healing in personal reflection time alone.

But this night was different. I glanced around, anxious, hoping I would not recognize anyone as I sat alone.

The place was hip, vibrant, and a refreshing change from some of the more laid back, iconic family-friendly restaurants which spotted our neighborhood community. The small outdoor patio, while facing a parking lot, still created a sense of freedom that I enjoyed in our sea of concrete sprawling throughout Dallas.

That's why I faced my fears of being seen alone—because of the comfort of the energy there. I wanted to experience a vibe to pep me up a bit.

But as I sat there, my worry increased that someone would see me sitting alone.

LONELINESS CAN CREATE A DOWNWARD SPIRAL KEEPING US STUCK

My thoughts began to spin. *If I make eye contact with someone I know, will they feel the need to come up and talk to me? Will they feel sorry for me and say something awkward? Will I have to be jovial and nonchalant? Do I have to ask them about their kid's games this week?*

The voices in my head were in full chatter.

Or, one of the others proposed, *what if it's one of the women I know who is unhappy in her marriage or with her life? Will she act catty, perhaps jealous that she is not able to get time alone to herself?*

When the server came to my table, I was not even aware of her presence. "Can I get you something to drink?" she asked politely.

But I was far away in my made-up land of loneliness.

What is wrong with you? I asked myself judgmentally. *Just a few months ago, you spent almost a week by yourself traveling to Florida for a beach getaway. What's so bad about this?*

And it was at that moment looking up at the waitress—who was likely wondering if I was hard of hearing—I realized it: I felt lonely.

BRINGING AWARENESS TO LONELINESS THROUGH EMPATHY CREATES CONNECTION

My worry about what others thought about me (the others who were not even there except in my head) put me into a spiral of lonely feelings.

It was an odd awareness. For me, this awareness of "feeling lonely" was new. I did not identify with "being lonely." From the time I was young, I had many friends. I never had to be alone because I could easily surround myself with people.

If you are familiar with the Clifton Strength Finder assessment by Gallup, it helps identify the areas where you have (or your team has if used in that context) the greatest potential to use or build strengths. I have personally found it helpful to increase happiness. The more I use my strengths, the happier I feel. My number one strength is WOO (Winning Others Over) and my second strength is "Empathy." These top two strengths create an easy path of connection, one where I can immediately connect and enjoy a meaningful connection with almost everyone I meet.

But those two strengths did not leave a lot of room for my own emotions. That night, I began to realize how "self-opaque" I have been as a result—aware of others' feelings but unaware of my own.

Something shifted in my self-knowledge as I wondered about what others thought of me. I felt the depth of my loneliness. And I realized no one is immune to feeling lonely, not even me— someone who had managed to avoid that feeling for most of her life. For maybe the first time ever, I started to understand what loneliness felt like. I remembered an exercise I had just conducted in a focus group the day before where we were trying to access consumers' feelings about their mid-day snacks. It was a sentence stem they filled out to better understand emotions when eating different snacks:

"I feel _____ (emotion) when _____ (occasion) because _____ (I am thinking)."

So as if I was a member of my own focus group, I pulled out a pen and paper and decided to do the exercise for myself.

I feel <u>lonely</u> when <u>I am sitting at a place where I used to feel connected</u> because <u>I am thinking about seeing the smile on my daughter's face and she's not here. I miss her.</u>

Wow! Didn't see that coming! My loneliness was derived from missing the specific connection with my daughter, not necessarily the idea of being alone. And then I realized that my over-scheduled life of work, parenting, kid's activities, community, and church activities did not leave a lot of room to feel anything. All of the commitments and obligations had created a void of being in touch with what was really going on inside. When I finally had a chance to connect with myself, I didn't want to. I didn't want to feel what I had been avoiding, the discomfort of feelings was easy to push aside.

Sometimes the successful life I've built is one that doesn't allow me to even breathe or feel anything. So, after breathing through this feeling of loneliness, another thought hit me. This time it was a question, not a judgmental one like the earlier ones, but one of curiosity. *If I could connect with anyone right now, who would that be?*

At first, the voice who answered said, *No one. You don't have anyone who would understand you right now.*

But then, a softer gentler voice—the voice of empathy— said something surprising. *I wonder how Sarah is doing. I remember she had surgery last week and I never heard how it went.*

And with that, I picked up my phone and dialed Sarah's number. As I connected with myself, I was able to flow through the temporary feeling of loneliness and connect outside of me, not for me or about me, but for her.

That was when I realized the clarity that comes from becoming aware of feelings without judging them, just letting them be. From that place, I was allowed room to breathe through the human experience of emotion. I had created that space to observe thousands of times for those who expressed their feelings to me in a focus group or interview. And I had just created that space from within. It was a game changer because in my connection to self, I was able to exhibit more empathy for someone I cared about.

Our thoughts create our emotions and our emotions create our reality. Learning to be with and move through emotion instead of staying stuck in it allows us to take one step toward what we desire to create.

CONNECTED TEAMS CREATE BETTER TOGETHER

I have noticed in our innovation projects over the years a common theme amongst the most successful teams. They have a humorous, synergetic relationship. Often it is sarcastic humor, but nonetheless, they have fun. They see the crazy unknown as a game of learning together. They exhibit comradery and a collaborative team spirit. I watch them enjoy time together outside of work and observe them gently making fun of each other. They laugh because they know things about each other's personal lives. They understand one another holistically and "have each other's back." They know they can rely on the team in times of need.

OVERWORKED TEAMS BREED LONELINESS AND APATHY FOR INNOVATION

The problem I have increasingly witnessed is that most affluent corporate employees have so much pressure and workload with their demanding jobs that they do not have time to find the humor and fun in the work they do. And if they are not using the social connecting skills of "gamifying" a creative project together, they can lose connection. Once teams lose emotional and personal connections, they often begin competing to prove themselves individually rather than working together to create together. And competition breeds loneliness because we experience loneliness when we believe others will hurt, not help, us.

LONELINESS IMPACTS INNOVATION WHEN TEAMS LOSE THE SPIRIT OF "WE"

When teams or organizations feel like they have to compete to succeed, it creates a downward spiral and a culture of loneliness. Loneliness impacts innovation because it keeps individuals stuck instead of connected and creating together.

This makes loneliness one of the least talked about problems impacting organizational innovation. When individuals on a team feel connected through play, they work better together. While corporate leaders may enjoy affluence, they are also more socially disconnected due to the lack of time for meaningful connections to grow.

In fact, studies show that the affluent could be the lone-liest. Researchers from Emory University and the University of Minnesota analyzed survey responses from nearly 120,000 Americans, honing in on questions about annual household income and social behavior. Their results showed that people with higher incomes spent less time socializing, and more time alone, overall. Higher income creates the opportunity to pay for services that lower-income people use their social networks for: things like childcare, rides to the airport, or home maintenance. Emily Bianchi of Emory University and Kathleen Vohs of the University of Minnesota say there's a fairly robust body of research showing that "having or thinking about money appears to heighten self-reliance and dampen attention and responsiveness to others" (Simon-Thomas, 2016).

EMPATHY FOR SELF AND OTHERS IS A SALVE FOR LONELINESS

Loneliness was on the rise before COVID, and due to the impact of it, it has continued to increase. In 2020, 61 percent of Americans reported they felt lonely, and more than a third reported feeling a general sense of empti-ness or disconnection from others when they are at work (Unger, 2021).

But a study published in *Aging and Mental Health* jour-nal found that people are less lonely when they embrace uncertainty and feel empathy. The researchers at the University of California San Diego School of Medicine's

Center for Healthy Aging built a scale they call the San Diego Wisdom Scale which measured six factors of "wisdom":

1. empathy and compassion,
2. emotional regulation,
3. self-reflection,
4. accepting uncertainty and diversity,
5. decisiveness, and
6. advice given.

In four separate studies across different cultures and age groups, the team found an inverse correlation between loneliness and "wisdom." Those who were high on the "wisdom" scale were less lonely. Wisdom derived from exhibiting and demonstrating both self and other empathy can become a protective factor from loneliness (Michelson, 2020).

I have experienced through my work, in study after study, that when people can express their feelings without worry of being judged for them, they move out of loneliness into gratitude. When you connect with someone, really listen to them, and they can express themselves fully, they are less lonely because they feel seen and heard.

We are grateful when we are seen and heard because that is our deepest longing. And with a grateful heart, the lonely want to give back. Connection leads to gratitude and gratitude leads to more connection—that's the upward spiral.

CREATING FOR OTHERS CONNECTS US AND SOLVES LONELINESS

Before she said it, I could sense her discomfort. "...It's because I feel less lonely. When I bake cakes for others, I feel connected to them. Like I am creating something they love."

There were seven of us sitting around the table for this focus group, all women. I had been exploring the experience and emotions of cake bakers. The room had been transformed into a living room, to help create psychological safety. I was in a large, comfortable gray-suede chair with side arms I could rest into. The more at ease they felt, the faster it would be to facilitate a meaningful discussion.

She began to gesture as she went on, "I especially love baking cakes when we have a big family gathering. Sometimes I struggle to make conversation with my family. My life is so different than my mom's. I don't think she understands the work stress I have. Mom stayed home with us when we were growing up. She taught me how to bake, some of my favorite memories. I still enjoy it because it's my way of giving back. It's a break from my reality and I feel more connected once it's done."

The other women chimed in. And it appeared she was not alone. While each woman in the room had a different version, they all believed that "baking created connection" because it helped them connect and experience joy. As they left, the woman who had opened the conversation stopped and touched my arm and said, "Thank you!"

"Well, you're welcome, but for what?" I asked.

She said, "I never knew I felt that way and now, I want to bake even more. You helped me see what I couldn't just by letting me talk about why I love it."

I smiled brightly. As she left, I remembered a similar conversation only a few weeks before—about a completely different subject.

It had been in the backyard of a man just outside Charlotte, North Carolina. His name was Greg, age thirty-seven with three kids and a wife. He signed up for our study for barbecue meats. We had traveled across the states, visiting Kansas City, Austin, San Diego, and now Charlotte to understand the differences in process, sauces, and why that particular region's BBQ was "the best."

I was there at his house with two of my clients.

A billow of smoke swirled above us as he taught me all he knew about meat preparation. I was fascinated by everything I had learned in a week about grills, wood varieties, sauces, etc. But I was still learning. Curiously, I asked:

"What does barbecuing provide for you—what do you get out of it?"

He first answered, "I love it."

So I pressed, eager to understand. "Why do you love it so much?" And there it was—an emotional reaction I wasn't expecting.

He said almost the same words I had just heard from my cake baker: "I feel less alone when I am barbecuing. Sometimes, I don't know exactly how to engage in the table conversation, but I always know I belong with them when I've helped prepare what they're eating. I like the time alone while I'm preparing it. It gives me space to think and anticipate seeing everyone's faces as they wait to eat the meat I so carefully prepared. It's like I give each one of them a little bit of me."

Tears then filled his eyes. And with the back of his hand, grill tongs and all, he wiped a tear and went on to say, "Sometimes I get so caught up in my day-to-day work. By the time I look up, I realize I haven't connected with anyone in a meaningful way all day. Then my wife and I pass each other like ships in the night, rush around hauling kids around and fall into bed exhausted. Repeat. But when I am out here alone grilling or smoking meats, I can see why I'm doing everything else. And when I can take the time to remember that, I feel less lonely."

He was much more sentimental than my cake baker. I teared up that day, too as I felt what he did. Later, as we left, he hugged me with both arms and said, "Thank you. I enjoyed that." Then with a twinkle in his eyes, he said, "I gotta go check on the meat."

What I realized by both respondents revealing their emotion of loneliness is that through their creations, it allowed them to connect on a deeper level with others. We connect through what we create for others.

While loneliness can impact our innovation by keeping us stuck and isolated, it can also be a guiding light if we can remember the truth—we are not alone, and that what we create will help us connect more deeply with others. Our creations are the guiding light to the connection we are looking for.

FIRESTARTER SPARKS—EMPATHY TRANSFORMS LONELINESS TO CONNECTED GRATITUDE

1. Loneliness Can Create a Downward Spiral, Keeping Us Stuck
2. Bringing Awareness to Loneliness through Empathy Creates Connection
3. Connected Teams Create Better Together
4. Overworked Teams Breed Loneliness and Apathy for Innovation
5. Loneliness Impacts Innovation When Team Loses the Spirit of "We"
6. Empathy for Self and Others Is a Salve for Loneliness
7. Creating for Others Connects Us and Solves Loneliness

FIRESTARTER FUEL—IGNITING ME

1. What type of activities make you feel most connected to yourself?
2. Where could you carve time for these activities into your schedule? When will you do that?
3. When, where, and why do you feel most connected to others?
4. When do you experience loneliness? What triggers it?

FIRESTARTER FUEL—IGNITING WE

1. Who could you build a connection with at work to give you more joy or fun or a more meaningful connection?
2. What interests do you have in your career that you could pursue?
3. What would you create at work that would provide more commitment to your work?

CHAPTER 11

RIGIDITY

I grimaced as the long, thick intramuscular needle penetrated my right hip. The flood of progesterone created the immediate yet slow and steady burn I had grown accustomed to. Even though I traded which hip would get the stab, I looked down and saw the bruise that wouldn't go away.

We had just finished the final focus group of the day. My client discarded the needle efficiently and safely in the travel recyclable bag I had carried for our project. Without saying a word, we exited the back room of the focus group facility. The other two team members smiled warmly and said, "Are you okay, April?"

I nodded, still amazed at their generosity. Their ability to move through what felt like reversed roles on this project made me more uncomfortable than it did them.

It was 2009 and, after almost two years of fertility treatments, I was finally pregnant. I was six weeks into taking progesterone shots to stay that way when I got a call from a client and good friend.

"April, I neeeed you on this project," she implored after I told her that I didn't know if I could take it on.

She was hard to say no to, amazingly brilliant and beautiful, she was a dream to work with, and she clearly knew how to work my ego!

She wanted to conduct research in two cities—San Francisco and Chicago—which would mean a full five days of twelve hours or more, including city-to-city travel. Our days were long, each one a series of two-hour focus groups combined with work sessions to unravel and discern the most meaningful learnings surrounding the subject. This time it was coffee.

I was in a conundrum. I was taking hormone shots twice a day, trying to maintain the internal environment necessary for the fetus growing inside me to continue developing.

My mind scrambled, working to solve what was possible logistically, knowing that with our early start days and late evenings, it would be a challenge to figure out when, where, and how I might be able to inject my twice-daily shots.

My strongest desire was to give birth to this baby. And I also desired to keep what I had already birthed the year before: my budding business. I wanted to keep my new business running, make my clients happy, and be available to help them bring their products to life.

Up until that point, my husband had been giving me the shots each morning and evening. And as much as I wanted to be self-reliant, I couldn't force my hands to deliver the shots to myself. I had a deep fear of needles. Mustering the courage for three months of needles, twice a day was hard enough in the comfort of my home. But I was committed if it meant a greater chance of birthing my baby.

I told her I would look at my calendar and see what I could figure out. As I hung up the phone, I went through my typical analysis on how to solve this client's problem and bend myself to meet her needs. The challenge was this: I did not know if or how to be vulnerable with my clients. *I cannot tell them what is really going on for me*, I told myself.

RIGIDITY LIMITS OUR ABILITY TO CREATIVELY PROBLEM SOLVE

My very ingrained belief that my job was to serve them, and their job was to pay me for serving them was a transactional way of thinking of the relationship. If I give x, they will give y. Anything other than that was not acceptable in my mind at the time. That was the rigid belief system that caused me sleepless nights the next two days. I knew I was in a situation that was butting me up against my beliefs. It was an either/or, win/lose mentality.

But something shifted when I began to express my problem to a friend. I opened with: "I have this problem. A client wants me to do a project. She's with a new company and it would be great for me to get the experience and renew my relationship with her at her new company. And I really want to help her succeed there. But I have to stay home to get my shots twice a day. I would never forgive myself if I made the choice to go and lost the baby because of it."

My friend looked at me without saying a word for a good sixty seconds, then said, "I have a question. If you could have a magic wand, what would you want to happen? What would be ideal for you?" (Ironically, this is something we ask in groups a lot, so I appreciated the question.)

"Well," I said slowly as I thought about it, "I would take the work and bring the progesterone with me and have her give me the shots." Then I chuckled, "But of course I can't do that. I can't ask her to give me shots in my ass! That would be crazy. I'm sure that's against some kind of client/vendor rule anyway."

But my friend smiled and said, "Why don't you ask her and find out?"

Again, with rigidity, I denied this as a viable possibility. So, she said, "Look. Don't ask her if it makes you uncomfortable. You need to do what gives you the most comfort so if you want to stick to two choices, you can either:

1. not take the project or
2. take the project and risk the baby"

And that is when I recognized my friend's wisdom, enough to hug her right there across our salads. Instead of giving me the pros and cons of each or trying to convince me of one choice being the clear winner, she so brilliantly opened my eyes to something new. She helped me see that my own beliefs about how I had to be with my clients were blinding me. My lack of vulnerability had created a sense of separation, which kept me stuck rather than creating what I really desired: the ability to keep both my growing baby and business safe. Her empathic question helped me see new possibility.

LETTING GO OF RIGID BELIEFS CREATES POSSIBILITY

So, I picked up the phone the next day, and called my client back. And with what felt like a great deal of vulnerability, I said, "I can do the project, but I need someone to give me a shot in the hip every night we are gone. I'm pregnant and the doctor is insisting I take two shots of progesterone a day."

And without missing a beat, in her calm, poised voice and problem-solving demeanor she said, "Not a problem, April. I'm not the one to do it because shots make me queasy but the girl who works for me was raised on a ranch and I've heard her talk about giving cattle shots. I'll get her to do it."

And with a simple three-minute conversation, this large problem was solved. We went. We did the work. And every night after focus groups were over, this sweet young woman who had not even known me a few days earlier efficiently pulled out the needle while I lowered my pants and shot progesterone into me with the nonchalant demeanor of a well-trained nurse. It was quick, simple, and easy.

And so it went. Just a couple of weeks later, another one of my beloved, brilliant, and beautiful clients asked me to go on a project to study women's hair care in New York. And with my new beliefs and enthusiasm to break free from my rigid beliefs, I ventured into this uncomfortable conversation again.

"Yes, I would love to do the project, but in order to do that, would you consider giving me two shots each day, morning and night, while we are traveling?"

Nonplussed and eager to help, she said, "Not only is this not a problem, April, I would be honored to help you." She had a second job as a paramedic and firefighter, so it didn't even phase her. She was so gracious that she also helped me create a project schedule for our work to allow the extra time for my shots. Every morning before our research and again at night in our high-rise hotel in New York, she came to my hotel room, gave me my progesterone shot as if she was delivering a toothbrush, and it was done. Success. Win/win.

The beauty of letting go of rigidity is that it allows us to grow. Like a lizard that regenerates lost extremities, when we allow new beliefs to enter and adapt our thinking, possibility arises as if by magic.

I honestly did not know I was rigid; I used to pride myself on my own adaptability and flexibility to bend for my clients. But the rigidity came from believing that there was only one way to be with them in the relationship. Once I became clear about what I needed, I allowed a more in-depth relationship to occur. A relationship that to this day has continued to grow with both of these women, as clients and friends.

Rigid thinking means an inability to change your mind when all signs point to a much-needed change of mind. It also implies an inability to see a situation from a different point of view. People with rigid thinking see life with blinders on, perceiving only one out of the countless nuances there are (Exploring your mind, 2021).

Rigidity occurs because we have dedicated ourselves to our beliefs. Rigidity keeps us stuck in the same situation. If the situation works, rigidity is our friend. But when we are faced with a decision or a sudden change of direction—one where we cannot seem to see the way through to the other side—it's likely due to letting our beliefs instead of our desires drive us. Rigid thinking makes us feel like we're constantly messing up because we're not conforming to the beliefs in our mind. Thus, we feel guilt, anxiety, and uselessly overthink when our beliefs have a stronghold on us.

CREATIVITY COMES WHEN WE MOVE FROM RIGIDITY TO MENTAL AGILITY

But the opposite of rigidity is soft, gentle, flexible, malleable. Often these words come with a lot of baggage. Many of us received messages that the way to succeed is to "be tough" and "power through." We often reject the idea of softness as a path to success. But from a neuroscientific lens, our adaptation and ability to succeed is through plasticity. Neuroplasticity (or brain plasticity), according to neuroscientists, is the ability for the brain to "rewire" itself—to change and adapt in response to learning and experience.

What if we reframed our rigidity to mental agility? Could we become more creative in our approach to innovative problem solving?

According to Eric Maisel, PhD, author of *Brainstorm: Harnessing the Power of Productive Obsessions* and numerous other books, we can. "Rigid, 'black and white' thinking can help to eliminate some stress-producing details," he says. "But that doesn't make us deep thinkers or creative. It doesn't allow us to deal with problems easily when they arrive. Rigid thinking does help us make quick decisions about things, but it's not suited to help us with our lifestyle."

It's easier, for example, to pick one position; to be against the war or in favor of lower taxes, for instance, instead of evaluating the complexities and recognizing that war sometimes has positive outcomes and that lower taxes aren't always for the best.

Wilma Koutstaal, PhD, psychologist at the University of Minnesota and the author of the book *The Agile Mind* says about rigidity: "It can enable us to be more effective problem solvers and problem finders, helping to foster creativity and innovation, and allowing us to identify and realize promising opportunities."

"Sometimes you can get a lot of mileage from being highly specific, and that's a good thing," Koutstaal says. "But sometimes you need to be way more abstract to adapt to the situation."

She goes on: "Mental flexibility is really about adaptability and our ability to shift our thoughts between the abstract and specific in order to respond effectively to any given situation."

A flexible mindset moves us away from limiting thought patterns to a place of openness and possibility. In those moments, when you are feeling stuck, worn out by the regular routine or caught in old habits and repetitive patterns, you can adapt your thinking and behavior in a way that will inspire you and boost your resilience and your chance at success.

When we're feeling happy or optimistic, for example, we tend toward broad and inclusive thinking. When we're able to make that mental shift without remaining stuck in a particular mindset, we're demonstrating mental flexibility.

IMAGINATION MOVES US FROM MENTAL RIGIDITY TO AGILITY

And one way to create plasticity in the brain is to use our imagination. When my friend asked, "What would you want if you had a magic wand?" she brought me into a state of imagination. I had to move out of "figuring it out" and into my heart to begin to visualize what an ideal scenario would "look like" for me.

Norman Doidge, in his book *The Brain That Changes Itself: Stories of Personal Triumph from the Frontiers of Brain Science* says: "One reason we can change our brains simply by imagining is that, from a neuroscientific point of view, imagining an act and doing it are not as different as they sound. When people close their eyes and visualize a simple object, such as the letter A, the primary visual cortex lights up, just as it would if the subjects were actually looking at the letter A. Brain scans show that in action and imagination many of the same parts of the brain are activated. That is why visualizing can improve performance."

When you get to see people who are phenomenal at using their imagination in action, it can be transformative. For me, that's what happened when I met Bob Goff, *New York Times* bestselling author of *Love Does* and *Everybody Always* and *Dream Big*.

As I drove up the two-mile driveway at The Oaks retreat center, I was a little nervous. Just a few days before, another friend forwarded an email to me from Bob Goff that simply said: "You need to do this."

If it wasn't from her, I would have ignored it but after three nights of "sleeping" (or lack of sleeping) on it, I decided to take her suggestion and invest in the Writer's Retreat at Bob's center. This was during what we thought was the tail end of COVID, and things had opened up enough to do a small retreat with all the precautions in place.

That first night after gathering the twenty-five of us aspiring authors, he began to pour into us, asking us to join him around one of the immaculate rock-built campfires. Our rocking chairs created a gentle rhythm that mirrored the cadence of his words. I was lulled in by the surroundings and setting. The companionship, connection, and warmth we felt lit up the place with fire dancing in our center. Nestled in Southern California, about two hours east of San Diego amongst beautiful rolling hills, the 240-acre retreat center was a place of paradise.

While much of his inspirational message came from his experience and knowledge of the publishing industry, something he said brought me back from the *gezellig* (Dutch for cozy and warm) feeling I was experiencing. His words surprised me as he said them with a contagious, effervescent, joy-filled statement, "I didn't realize when I bought this in 2019 that COVID would happen. It put a damper on the economics since we couldn't really do the retreats as we expected." He chuckled at the thought.

I did a double take. I couldn't figure out what was funny but then I understood the magic he was creating in his life. This is the same magic I know works for my clients when they innovate and design incredible products and services.

He said, "I just looked around me one day and saw there was land for vineyards and others were growing grapes. Also, I noticed there was a horse race track next door. Guess what? I have a practice track here on the property. So, instead of focusing on what wasn't working, I started studying these things that were adjacent to me. So, I just adapted the way I was thinking about it."

He used the power of his imagination coupled with adjacency (what was near but unrelated) to creatively solve—an agile mind.

I laughed with him now, seeing the irony in my epiphany. *Yes*, I thought, *SCAMPER: Substitute, Combine, Adapt, Modify, Put to Another Use, Eliminate, Rearrange.* He used one of the tools we use in our corporate ideation sessions all the time. He did it here in his own life. He began to design something using the adaptability of the brain to see opportunity; possibility when you are open to it.

He pulled me back in again as he continued to talk about what had transpired. "So, it wasn't long after I realized training racehorses might be a good idea when a friend called and asked me if I wanted to buy a horse for one dollar because it was not useful due to an injury. So, I said sure. Then guess what happened—when I traced the lineage, it turns out she's the granddaughter of Seabiscuit!"

Now he had us going. We were barreling over with laughter by the time he told us his vineyard story. "I've never had a drop of wine but I'm growing grapes now for a vineyard. Who knew?" he said, with his exaggerated grin. Even behind his big glasses, I could see his eyes were smiling.

And so were mine. Bearing witness to see possibility arise by watching someone who had used his brain's neuroplasticity and imagination was an inspiration. Not only did he motivate me with his story, but he also saw an opportunity to help me get unstuck out of my own rigidity.

MENTAL AGILITY IS ACTIVATED THROUGH EMPATHY

The next morning while I was getting coffee, he joined me and asked a simple question: "What do you need help with?" I answered with a complicated set of ideas, conundrums, and worries based on my beliefs. He blinked slowly as he listened. And when I finished, he said with warmth in his eyes, "Go take a seven-day retreat and finish the book, April. Everything else will get sorted out in your head in due time."

In my two biggest "innovations" in my personal life, I noticed a common thread. Someone listened to understand the emotional problem I was trying to solve. With empathy, they helped me untangle my own thinking. In both cases, my personal rigidity was released by empathy because my eyes were open to seeing more than I could before. That is the power of empathy.

Innovation begins when imagination arises by asking questions that allow us to reflect on what we believe. Beliefs take you back to the results you already have. Beliefs are the source of your current results. Imagination creates a pathway to give you access to the results you want.

With practice and awareness, we can develop an agile mind that will elevate our experience and help us live more resilient, creative, happy lives, and ultimately, create more meaningful innovation.

FIRESTARTER SPARKS—EMPATHY TRANSFORMS RIGIDITY TO MENTAL AGILITY

1. Rigidity Limits Our Ability to Creatively Problem Solve
2. Letting Go of Rigidity Creates Possibility
3. Creativity Comes When We Move from Rigidity to Mental Agility
4. Imagination Moves Us from Mental Rigidity to Agility
5. Mental Agility is Activated through Empathic Questioning

INDIVIDUAL FIRESTARTER FUEL—IGNITING ME

1. What situation are you in that you want to see differently?
2. What are your beliefs about this?
3. What else is possible beyond what you already know?
4. What/where/when can you learn something new about this subject?

5. Who has a different opinion that you could listen to and learn from?

TEAM FIRESTARTER FUEL—IGNITING WE

1. How have we been approaching this situation thus far?
2. Where are we stuck? What are the beliefs around the situation?
3. What and where could we learn outside of the organization as a new way to think about our current problem?

CHAPTER 12

OVERWHELM

"What did you say, Jeremy?" he screamed from through the phone. "I don't think I heard you right. Did you say your spot price was the SAME AS YESTERDAY?" Each syllable was louder than the one before. "Are you lazy or just dumb?"

Jeremy stammered, frozen in fear. "Well, uh, we based this on yesterday's closing prices and, uhhh..." It was 8:30 a.m. and our small grain elevator's trading floor had been buzzing with excitement in anticipation for the markets to open until the dreaded 8:30 call that came in on the bright red phone connecting all the grain elevators along the Mississippi River. We were as silent as church mice now.

Enraged with my friend Jeremy's lack of clarity, the voice on the other side of the red phone hotline pumped up the volume. "Can someone who knows what they're doing down there in Mount Vernon get on the damn phone?" The voice was the lead trader up in Chicago. The desk traders at the Chicago Board of Trade were intelligent and experienced. Their skills baffled the rest of us new hires. New hires were put in the grain elevators along the Mississippi to "learn the ropes."

We looked around at each other like a bunch of sheep waiting to be slaughtered. No one moved. Finally, our manager came to our rescue.

Nothing scared me more than those dreaded 8:30 a.m. "hotline" calls.

"Sir, everything is fine down here." And in an overly confident tone, he gave him our spot price.

We were not the only elevator that would get raked over the coals. I felt like I knew every voice, every name on those calls although none of us had ever met. We had a shared experience because of them—some might call that shared experience PTSD.

OVERWHELM OCCURS WHEN PRESSURE SEEMS GREATER THAN RESOURCES

As the day continued, my overwhelm increased. I was twenty-three, and his anger earlier had set us all on edge, especially those of us who were new. When our manager got off the phone, his calm confidence transformed into heated rage. We were not sure if he was mad at us or the lead trader who had just shamed him in front of his entire staff. But he walked hurriedly into his office, slammed the door, and stayed on his private phone the rest of the morning. He was yelling more than talking.

We couldn't hear every word, but we could see everything. Nothing was private due to the floor-to-ceiling glass walls and door. And his powerful exertion of anger had me looking at him more than my computer screen. I was facing him, and even from a distance, I could sense his demeanor was not calming down. My feeling of overwhelm did not settle either.

That was the day it happened: I made a really bad trade. My job was to buy physical grain from farmers at the lowest possible trading price and then "hold" the grain until I could sell it when the prices lifted based on the Chicago Board of Trade pricing. The trick was to not only build relationships so that farmers would want to trust your guidance and then sell to you, but also to ensure you sold that grain at a profit.

But that day, I did not make a profit. I made a loss for the company. The training mentality had been a sink or swim education. When I started, my first manager pointed to the green trading screen on my desk filled with lines of numbers moving rapidly, slammed a Rolodex of potential customers to contact and said: "Buy low and sell high. Now, get to work."

That was my training ground. So here we were, a few months in, after a quick promotion from my first grain elevator, I was overwhelmed talking to one farmer ready to sell, two others waiting, when the market spiked. I acted fast, determined to get the grain purchased.

In my hurry, I settled on an incorrect price, and it wasn't until about an hour later when I was finalizing the paperwork, that I realized I had bought high and sold low. In essence, I lost a significant amount of money for the company—in a matter of seconds. It was a bad trade.

My heart sank. I sat frozen for almost thirty minutes, then went to the bathroom, vomited, and silently with my head held higher than I felt started down the dreaded path through the walkway of my peers' desks into my boss' office. Their eyes followed me, darting back and forth, heads turning in my direction as I moved past them.

As I knocked on the glass door, I could see his irritation. His mood was less than pleasant. But I told him anyway:

"I have something to tell you. I made a bad trade."

"How bad?" He eyed me warily. "You know I have zero patience for stupid people."

I swallowed. "Bad. I sold a barge worth of grain (55,000 bushels) for ten cents under what I purchased it for. It's a $5,500 loss." I choked as I said it, willing myself not to cry as I told him. I went on, not able to stop myself, "I was just so overwhelmed. Three people were on the line and the market was moving fast. I made the mistake because my brain couldn't think straight in my rush. I'm sorry."

He breathed heavily and then to my surprise, as he exhaled, he gestured for me to sit down in the chair facing him. Then he said something I'll never forget. It was surprising coming from this man who I couldn't imagine being soft.

He said, "April, it's time for you to learn an equation every good trader knows about overwhelm. Overwhelm is when your brain is under too much stress. Here is a formula to remember. Burn this one into your brain along with the one you forgot today of Buy Low and Sell High. Stress occurs when Pressure is greater than Resources ($S = P > R$). The key to good trading is to emotionally regulate your actions under pressure. And you do that by finding ways to decrease pressure while increasing your resources."

LESSEN OVERWHELM IN THE UNKNOWN BY SLOWING DOWN INSTEAD OF SPEEDING UP

I looked at him, confused. He realized his words did not compute.

He waited for a question so he could direct the instruction correctly. So I asked,

"What do you mean by pressure? How can I reduce it? It is what it is. I can't do anything about all of the things flying in at the same time. So, how can I possibly reduce the pressure I'm feeling?"

"You just answered your own question," he said. "The pressure you need to focus on reducing is internal, not external pressure."

I argued, "But I can't reduce the pressure inside with all of the external pressure."

He continued, "Okay, let's say hypothetically you could have chosen to focus on only one thing. Out of all the things you were doing, what would have had the greatest impact, opportunity, or value to you if you only did that one thing?"

I thought about it. "I guess it would be ensuring I bought the farmer's grain at the moment they were all wanting to sell."

"Why?" he pressed.

I answered, "Because I knew it would make you happy with me to receive the grain. They were all three new customers, which is important not just short-term but long-term."

"Right," he said. "Yes, I agree. By the way, great job on getting three new customers. You could have led with that, by the way. Now, what made you rush to sell?"

"I was completely stressed after the market took an unexpected turn, and I was scared that if I didn't sell then, things would get worse, so I scrambled to sell before things got worse."

"What resources did you have available?"

Dumbfounded, I couldn't think of any.

"Who works in the front office and what is her job?" Suddenly, I remembered Tara. She was in charge of placing all of the sale orders. I had forgotten it wasn't my responsibility to put the sale orders in, just to give her guidance to do it. I remembered I had felt compelled to just finish the trade myself so that it was "done right." It would have relieved my pressure if I had slowed down, handed the purchase slip to her with some instruction. I could have focused on what I was good at, talking to customers and making them feel comfortable with their initial transaction with us.

Okay, I could see it. If I had slowed down and focused on the impact of what was most important to me, it would have reduced my internal pressure. And if I had seen the resources available, it would have further turned my stress equation around.

And then once he realized I understood, his normal grimace returned and gruffly he said: "Now get out there and clean up your mess." And then, just to ensure he had made his point, stated, "And if I were you, I wouldn't make that same mistake again because next time I'll fire you." And that was that. As I walked out, he pushed a button on his red hotline phone, activating the intercom. "Sally, get me John. One of the new hires made a bad trade down here and we need to offset it on the floor."

I discovered from one of my peers later that my huge mistake was quite small in the grand scheme of the company operations.

When I got to my desk, I wrote the equation and what it meant on a sticky note and attached it to my computer screen.

Stress = Pressure > Resources.

And I wrote another:

Peace = IR > EP. Peace = Internal Resources > External Pressure.

Then: SLOW DOWN, APRIL

EMPATHY CULTIVATES RESILIENCE BY TRANSFORMING OVERWHELM TO PEACE

I learned a lesson that continues to be a challenge to implement primarily because the pressure of higher expectations, more demanding work, and more commitments has created the need for more resources to keep stress at bay. The biggest downfall for most of us who have high-stress, demanding jobs is that we forget that external and internal pressure are not the same. How we handle pressure internally is the key to peace.

Navigating the complex web of tasks in ourselves takes deep connection to ourselves and others. And our resource for that is empathy.

Empathy is the pathway out of the unending overwhelm when innovating or creating change. When we allow ourselves to uncover our response to pressure or how we are applying pressure, we can set better boundaries and expectations that empower us.

Whether it's the sheer volume of information, or expectations and pressure coming at us from our various commitments, or perhaps the pressure we put on ourselves to perform, overwhelm is a part of today's hyper-connected culture.

When feeling overwhelmed, it's because we think or feel lacking in the ability, time, or resources to do what is in front of us.

But even in the greatest overwhelming moments of our lives, and especially when we are innovating, we have available internal resources that, when tapped into with empathy, can move us from overwhelm and into a more powerful place.

Rick Hanson, author of *Neurodharma*, expands on this idea of peace or "resilient well-being" by describing seven qualities that can free our minds back to truth:

1. Steadying the Mind
2. Warming the Heart
3. Resting in Fullness
4. Being Wholeness
5. Receiving Nowness
6. Opening into Allness
7. Finding Timeliness

Empathetic investigation increases our capacity to enhance these qualities as internal resources because when our brain slows down to observe and reflect on the cause of overwhelm, we can see new possibilities in these moments. This returns us to a state of peace so that our actions are focused and intentional.

Almost twenty-three years later, I had a new, unexpected trading experience. This one was even more overwhelming, and it gave me the opportunity to use the equation my manager had given me. Here's how empathy served to bring me back to peace during overwhelm.

INNOVATION CAN CREATE THE PERFECT STORM, LEADING US TO OVERWHELM

Fast forward to 2020. I found myself at a crossroads after a personal failure of a divorce. After lots of therapy, I started making the connections between my professional use of empathy to understand consumer behavior and my personal need for more "self-empathy." The idea of being kind to myself when I made mistakes was a new concept.

So, in my quest to reshape my life and relationships post-divorce, including the one with myself, I began writing each morning:

1. Five Gratitudes
2. Ten Future Dreams
3. One "Big" Current Goal

It was a surprise when, after only a couple of months my goal of finding a school where my daughter could thrive, I was also surprised with one of my "future" dreams.

In the process of finding and locating her school, I miraculously discovered a home on two acres with a barn and horse arena just five minutes from her school.

But like with any innovation, things do not always go as smoothly as you hope they will. The day after I committed under contract on both the house and the school, the market crashed—March 17th, 2020—tumbling to record lows due to COVID. At the same time, my business pipeline came to a screeching halt.

And the cash I had to cover my down payment was in a Fidelity equity account in blue-chip stocks. Because my money had been in equities, even though they were the best dividend-producing ones, I saw most of my money disappear in front of me. The money that remained in that account that day was a fraction of what it had been, barely enough to cover the down payment. Money flow halted. No more business on the horizon since most of my work was in person.

That evening, I noticed the overwhelm state I was in. And the theme of "not enough" danced in my head. And then, a memory emerged: the equation my boss had given me so many years earlier when I was in a situation of overwhelm with "not enough" time.

Stress = Pressure > Resources

and then the opposite,

Peace = Internal Resources > External Pressure

What are my resources? I asked myself with curious empathy. This question felt better than the ones I had been asking earlier that day. Things like, *what in the world am I going to do? How could you have made such a risky move?*

So I continued down this path of being with the situation asking and listening with empathy: *What is your goal, April? What will the value of this goal be to my daughter and me if I can get to the other side of it? What impact will it have on Autumn and me?*

These questions led me into further questioning: *What will I need to have in the bank to close on the house? What money do I need to get comfortable making house payments for six months if my business does not start back up? What resources do I have that I am not seeing?*

It was then I looked back at my online Fidelity account—the market had dropped further on the close. I did not know how to make trades. This account had been set up by my ex-husband to be a long-term "savings account." I had kept what we divided in the divorce untouched as if it would always increase. At the time, I believed that having a variety of blue-chip equity stocks would "never go down" but instead, steadily increase with a better interest rate plus dividend payouts than a normal savings account would.

As I went to bed that night, questions still swirled. *Should I take out what I have before it dwindles down to nothing? Do I opt out of the house? Do I save what little money I have to keep things afloat while we ride the storm?*

I thought back to the lessons I learned on the farm growing up when we were overwhelmed by hail or thunderstorms we could not have anticipated. I had been taught to mitigate risk so you can ride through any storm, no matter how bad it is.

But something new happened that evening for me. In the middle of the night, I woke up and wrote two words on a paper straight out of a dream: "Zoom" and "Clorox." The next morning, with complete confidence, I reached out to a friend who showed me the logistics of making a trade on the account. I pulled out the cash needed for the down payment, then sold everything else and bought as much Zoom and Clorox equity stock as I could with what remained.

I didn't realize it at the time, but empathic questioning took me from the overwhelm of *I don't know how, I don't have enough, How will I?* to new truths. It was answering the empathic questions that kept me attuned and able to emotionally manage through the fear and financial predicament I was in. I accepted it for what it was, and my brain created a solution.

EMPATHIC LISTENING MOVES US THROUGH OVERWHELM BY RETURNING US TO TRUTH

Sometimes we forget that the truth we seek already exists within us.

These were my truths I became aware of through attuning to myself:

1. Buy low and sell high.
2. Stocks rise fast when everyone needs or is using what is being sold
3. Everyone needed Clorox, and everyone was using Zoom
4. The school and house were a result of vision and faith
5. Faith always wins over fear

So, as I consciously chose to remove the voices in my head or in the news, I could reduce overwhelm and make choices in peace based on intentional internal truths instead. I listened to the wisdom driven by my heart.

"Have confidence and faith, April," I whispered to myself as I did it. "Accept this is where you are. And breathe into what you know. That will give you the confidence you need to do what you know to do. It's going to be okay." I continued to speak to myself empathetically.

That choice resulted in a profit, not a loss, for me. I beat all the market indexes rate of return in 2020 significantly. I was okay. And I gained confidence that I was not, in fact, a terrible trader, albeit many years later.

QUESTIONING THE TRUTH OF OVERWHELM MOVES YOU INTO FOCUSED ACTION

From that experience, I recognized what many psychologists are saying—that overwhelm is a byproduct of fear. Fear creates overwhelm because we can get stuck there: fight, flight, or freeze. This paralyzes us and removes our ability to act from a place of confidence or intention.

In their book, *Burnout,* Emily and Amelia Nagoski say, "We thrive when we have a positive goal to move toward, not just a negative state we're trying to move away from." Stress and overwhelm are not the problem, being stuck in them is.

And this is common when innovating because our brains are designed to be more confident with the known. We have to hijack our fear with empathy in order to move through the overwhelm that change brings.

A common acronym for fear is:

• FEAR—False Evidence Appearing Real

I developed a new acronym for FAITH to remind me of what I need to do with the lens of empathy to take me out of overwhelm and back into a more peaceful state:

• FAITH—Focused Action with Intentional Trust and Hope

When I am reminded that I can move out of overwhelm through a calm state of questioning the "truth," it brings me to greater truth. And that truth helps me take focused action that is intentional. When I make choices that are intentional and grounded in truth, away from a state of fear, I can flow back into clarity with confidence through faith.

FIRESTARTER SPARKS—EMPATHY TRANSFORMS OVERWHELM TO ACTING IN FAITH

1. Overwhelm Occurs When Pressure > Resources
2. Lessen Overwhelm in the Unknown by Slowing Down Instead of Speeding Up
3. Empathy Cultivates Resilience by Transforming Overwhelm to Peace
4. Innovation Can Create the Perfect Storm, Leading Us to Overwhelm
5. Empathic Listening Moves Us Through Overwhelm by Returning Us to Truth

FIRESTARTER FUEL—ME

1. What are you committed to?
2. What do you believe about others' expectations of you?
3. What is triggering your emotion of overwhelm or stress?
4. What resources are available to you?
5. What do you value that is getting compromised?

TEAM FIRESTARTER FUEL—WE

1. What is our goal? What are we committed to?
2. What pressure is unnecessary or causing a lack of productivity?

3. What could we focus on now that will make the most impact?
4. How could we reorganize our work so that it is better streamlined?
5. What would give us a sense of peace and a reason to celebrate?
6. What other resources might be available that we have not thought about?

PART III

THE AMPLIFIERS OF EMPATHY

Just as there are barriers to innovation, there are also amplifiers that help build empathy to create better innovation.

The purpose of this section is to give you some practical "ways of being" to help you increase your effectiveness at using empathy to innovate.

While the content here is only "scratching the surface" of this robust subject, I am including four qualities because they are the foundation to shift conversations and solve problems through the lens of empathy. These four qualities also correlate to what I have discovered at the heart of self-empathy and using empathy to innovate in relationships.

By practicing these qualities, I hope you will see yourself living more deeply connected and creative.

The first of these "amplifiers" is curiosity.

CHAPTER 13

CURIOSITY

It was a Friday night at seven o'clock, and I looked up suddenly from my mindless scrolling on my phone. I felt chills on the back of my neck. As my eyes looked beyond the comfort of the back living room couch where I was sitting, I saw a shadow swiftly move across the window of the front door.

I stealthily migrated from my seated position toward the kitchen bar, body bent over crouching so I could peer out without being seen as if that position would protect me. Curiosity overcame fear, as I tried to get closer to see who it was without them seeing me.

And then I saw him. A man I did not recognize—average height, middle-aged. And it didn't look as if he was dropping off an Amazon package. I waited a minute or so longer, hoping he would go away so I could get back to deciding whether I would watch my Netflix series or engage in my book. But no, he rang the damn doorbell again. I sighed, rolled my eyes, stood up from my crouch, and headed toward the door. As I moved that direction, wondering what in the world would bring a strange man to wait patiently outside, that's when I saw it.

I only cracked the door a bit, wondering if he was there to sell me on his religion. Little did I know, I wasn't far from the truth, but with an unexpected twist.

From the narrow opening in the door, I asked slightly irritated but politely, "Can I help you?" As he started to speak, a breeze blew it out of his hand. Further exasperated with the delayed gratification of knowing what the heck this guy was doing at my doorstep, I stood again waiting as he moved wildly across the porch trying to collect what he had been holding. As he started toward me again, he looked apologetic as he glanced at the letter he had been holding. He pushed it toward me and said: "My wife asked me to give this to you."

Not knowing what to say, my mind scrambled for answers to unspoken questions. *Is it laced with an explosive? Who is this man? Who is his wife? Why does she want to give this to me? And why did she use her husband to do so?* Most importantly, *People still hand deliver letters?* All the questions came at once, and finally, one escaped from the internal to the external world. "Who is your wife?"

As he said her name and I recognized it, I knew with a sick feeling that the contents of the letter would not be as rewarding as the Netflix show I was intent to watch. He handed it to me and shuffled away, without saying another word. I said, "Thank you," still bewildered.

SOMETIMES WE THINK WE KNOW THE ANSWER AND FORGET TO ASK IMPORTANT QUESTIONS

As I closed and locked the door behind him, I studied the envelope before willing myself to open it. I dreaded its contents. The letter began by expressing "deep sorrow of your pending divorce." She went on to say, "I am here for you" and "could we meet for coffee and talk?" And then the whammy: "I want you to know that God is not happy with your decision. Divorce is a sin in God's eyes, and I am absolutely convinced if you gave things over to God, and another try, you could make it work."

She went on to explain her logical "reasoning", but I had to stop reading after two pages. I hardly knew this woman and yet she seemed to "know" what was right for me, so much that she wrote me a letter telling me so, without ever asking and/or listening to me.

I sat shocked in disbelief. I couldn't find a place in my body to experience anything but numbness. I even poked my arm hoping I would feel something. That night, I let myself process what was going on in my body. By the next morning, I could see that my first emotion underneath the numbness was confusion but hidden below that was a deep well of anger as a recognition deep within started to take form.

Those who care because they think they "know the answer" without curiosity create walls between themselves and others.

WE CAN'T "FIX" BIG PROBLEMS UNTIL WE TRULY UNDERSTAND THEM

I noticed a lack of desire to understand me and instead a desire to "fix" me. The letter took me back to other friends and family who truly cared but were ultimately not helpful because they seemed to "know" more about my marriage than I did.

She was one of many who appeared to somehow have omniscient "knowledge" of what the problem was, even before they asked. Before that night, I had been contemplating if maybe they did know more than me. *Maybe they are right,* I had been thinking. *Maybe I need to pray or read the Bible more and this would be "fixed."* These were the swirling voices of reason I was drowning in.

Walls were being created all around me, shutting me out of the system I had tried so hard to fit into. I felt shut out because these "known" beliefs outweighed the desire to learn more from me by connecting to me and my heart. The only way to return to this knowing club was to abandon my own experience and truth.

Further, I realized in the space of finding my own truth that I did not want to step back into the world of the "known."

Those who knew could not be with me.

Those who cared and thought they knew how to solve my problem did not understand the problem.

I was starting a new path, into the unknown.

By allowing myself to venture into the unknown, a new world of possibility was created. I started finding other seekers, or maybe they found me. It wasn't long until an old friend of mine from high school reached out and wanted to get together. She not only asked how I was doing, but she also actually listened. An unexpected family member, my eighteen-year-old niece, appeared on my front step one day, curious. The difference between her and what I experienced above could be distilled into one word: curiosity. Instead of asking to validate their own beliefs of knowing, they wanted to listen to learn—deeply curious about my experience.

As I shared, my brain was able to experience the difference of what it was like to have someone curious about me instead of having someone judge me. Curiosity helped me work through my pain and put a healing salve to begin healing the wounds.

MIGRATING FROM KNOWING TO SEEKING WITH CURIOSITY HELPS US SOLVE FROM THE HEART

Curiosity carves a path out of pain because it helps us solve from the heart of our connection rather than the knowledge in our head.

I have continued to be surrounded by the curious, the open-hearted, almost daily. Or maybe I just notice them more now—now that I'm clear about how I feel in the presence of the curious. They are miraculous beings, these seekers; the ones curious and brave enough to venture out beyond what they "know."

I burned that letter the next day. I smiled with joy as I watched it burn, letting go of her judgment against me, her passive, all-knowing help delivered by her dutiful husband. I smiled, realizing no response was necessary from me.

I don't receive or respond to what is not mine to carry anymore. I receive other things, though: joy, love, kindness, and compassion; and these things come from those who are seekers exhibiting empathy.

The thing is this, it's easy to have empathy for people with similar circumstances and experiences. Other divorcees were quickest to come to my aid because they had a shared experience and could easily empathize.

CURIOSITY BUILDS EMPATHY BECAUSE IT'S A CONDUIT FOR CONNECTION

But it's damn hard to have empathy for people whose behaviors look like they go against your beliefs. The way to develop empathy when it's the most difficult is to cultivate curiosity. When you're curious instead of being judgmental about something you don't understand, you can build your empathy muscle. And building that muscle becomes easier because you can immediately see the benefit as new understanding arises.

There's a pattern of the curiosity characteristic in top CEO's called "Applied Curiosity." According to Adam Bryant, former *New York Times* "Corner Office" columnist, it's the most common characteristic that defines great leaders. Bryant interviewed 525 chief executives and other leaders over a ten-year span and found that applied curiosity is the single most important quality that explains why they all became CEOs. What's behind applied curiosity?

In Bryant's words: "It means trying to understand how things work, and then trying to understand how they can be made to work better. It means being curious about people and their backstories. It means using insights to build deceptively simple frameworks and models in their minds to make sense of their industry and all the other disruptive forces shaping our world so they can explain it to others. Then they continue asking questions about those models, and it's those questions that often lead to breakthrough ideas."

But curiosity is more than just a conduit to breakthrough ideas. Curious people create better connections. According to several studies published by Berkley's *Greater Good Magazine*, they reveal curious people have better relationships and connect better with others. People are more easily attracted and feel socially closer to individuals that display curiosity. Curiosity reduces group conflict, creates more open communication, and improves team performance.

Philosopher and psychologist William James, called it "the impulse towards better cognition," meaning it is the desire to understand what you do not know.

The more we get comfortable in habitual lines of work, the harder it is to break down beliefs that begin to form. We often take widely held opinions as facts. Research has shown that humans, unfortunately, are terrible at deciphering truth from fiction, even when presented with facts. People tend to believe that they know more than they do, and companies tend to reward people for "knowing" the answers. So, it creates a vicious cycle of knowledge generation rather than scientific curiosity.

Research by Dan Kahan, a professor of psychology at Yale University, found that "people with greater scientific curiosity are more likely to question surprising information, even if that information is contrary to their predispositions" (Dartmouth Engineering, 2020).

QUESTIONING INCONGRUENCE CURIOUSLY NOT ONLY BUILDS EMPATHY, IT ENHANCES INNOVATION

And that is why it is so much fun to use empathy to innovate with marketers and product developers. The great ones are those who are curious enough to question an incongruence rather than judge it. Here's a great example.

We walked up the steps to the stranger's door. There were four of us: three women and one man. The objective of this research was to deeply understand new moms and all of their emotional struggles, worries, and desires around being a new mom.

This type of behavioral research is called ethnography, where we utilize the art of observation like an anthropologist to learn behaviors, motivations, desires, and tensions in the context of people's homes. The result of learning in this way allows a marketing or product development team to better understand what is needed (we call this the "white space") in any given category. If they understand the gap—both physically and emotionally—they can create better solutions for consumers, because they deeply understand the subtle nuances.

Part of my job in these situations is to not only create a guide for the discussion so that the interview flows naturally, through observation but also focuses on what we want to learn. Also, setting up the conversation in a way that helps someone feel comfortable in their own home while strangers are observing or "studying" them is part of the art of creating the necessary conversation.

And this "psychological safety" need escalates when we're interacting with new moms and their babies. On this day we created a beautiful conversation with this mom. As she began to open up to us about what it was like to do and be all the things as a new mom, she teared up as she described the sometimes heavy emotions that plagued her on a daily basis: guilt for needing alone time, worry about the safety and care of the baby, exhaustion that turned into bitterness or anger when she didn't know how to stop the crying, then moments of pure joy when the baby was sleeping in her arms. We watched her as she watched her baby, talking to us unabashedly while rocking, shifting her position from seated to standing, seamlessly swaying her hips, flowing with the baby's cries and coos, still holding the conversation.

In this case, our insight arose after our mom respondent had been talking for an hour about how much she wanted all her baby products to be "natural." She talked about the importance of cloth diapers and other products being completely free of chemicals for her baby.

Then, her baby suddenly made it known he was hungry. She immediately went into the kitchen—all of us eagerly following to observe her behavior—opened the refrigerator, grabbed a jug of milk (adult, not baby milk), and began pouring it into the bottle. I think the baby was two months old. As she was doing this, I saw the team's eyes widen and one jaw drop in surprise. And I knew it was because there was an incongruence between her words of "desiring natural" and her behavior of choosing milk formulated for adults, not babies. It did not compute. As we all migrated back from the kitchen to the living room and she began feeding her baby this adult milk, the male marketing leader jumped in with a question: "Why are you feeding your baby adult milk?"

INNOVATIVE IDEAS ARE GENERATED WHEN WE GET CURIOUS ABOUT HUMAN IMPERFECTION AND INCONGRUENCY

I literally wanted to kick his ass in that moment. While I appreciated his curiosity, there's an art to getting people to open further, moving them from defending their behaviors to understanding them. And then I wanted to kick mine because clearly I had not prepped the team well enough in the art of questioning to learn more. I breathed really deeply and saw what I was afraid of as I looked at her shocked face.

She realized that her choice of milk for her baby impacted our opinion of her. As I scrambled to put a salve on the conversation, I rephrased to help a bit. "I think what he's wanting to understand is what milk do you consider most beneficial and least beneficial for your baby and why?"

She apologetically talked about what was going on in her mind. She said, "Well I don't usually give milk to my baby at all, because I feed him breast milk. But since all of you were here, I didn't feel comfortable doing that, so I just automatically wanted to stop the hungry cry and still keep you guys comfortable at the same time. I needed to make sure he was fed since he was hungry and that I could continue giving you what you needed."

It was so logical, resourceful, pragmatic.

In her situation, she couldn't think through what was best in that moment, given all she was trying to process with being there for us and her child at the same time. She had exhibited an almost childlike innocence. One of naïveté, albeit with good intention. It was innocent imperfection.

Resonating with imperfections creates a sense of compassion and desire to help or bridge the gap. This is the extraordinary lens that occurs when marketers are led to create a new product or message. Their desire comes from wanting to bridge the gap whether it's a gap of knowledge, belief, or what the consumer has versus what they desire. There's an inherent belief that we are all incongruent creatures and understanding the incongruencies and solving for those is where the magic lies because increased awareness coupled with a solution for what is hidden allows deeper emotional resonance in the value you offer.

The insight that arose was this: "natural" products were nice for a baby to have, but what mattered most was creating calm in the chaos. Life was chaotic for new moms, and they needed peace more than they needed "natural" products. But they wanted both natural products *and* peace. So the ideas and eventually the product line developed for this project shifted direction. Instead of "create a line of natural products" the lens was more nuanced: "create products that are natural and give a sense of peace." These are powerful implications for product innovation, because it's only when you understand the powerful emotional drivers that you creatively innovate.

CURIOSITY BUILDS COMPASSION FOR SELF AND EMPATHY FOR OTHERS

I experienced how a lack of empathy feels when others judge me, as was the case with the well-meaning Christian friend's letter. But it's ironic how many times I forget to observe without judgment in my personal life. I often lose sight of navigating my personal relationships with curiosity, including my relationship with myself.

When my own behaviors are not congruent with my desires, I can often get stuck in shame. But when I move to curiosity, identifying behaviors not as bad or wrong but as something I want to understand, I can shift.

When I put on the hat of wonder, I can see through a new lens: the lens of observation, curiosity, and listening to learn more. It is then that I can increase understanding by allowing myself to be aware of a belief, behavior, or habit, without the overlay of shame.

When we see ourselves as we are: innocent, imperfect human beings with good intentions, it can move us toward better solutions, because our brains are wired to want to "solve for a problem" or bridge the gap when we remove judgment. When we see others in the same way, it helps us tear down the wall and start building a bridge.

FIRESTARTER SPARKS—EMPATHY IS AMPLIFIED WHEN CURIOSITY BUILDS A BRIDGE

1. Sometimes We Think We Know the Answer and Forget to Ask Important Questions
2. We Can't Fix Big Problems Until We Truly Understand Them
3. Migrating from Knowing to Seeking with Curiosity Helps Us Solve from the Heart
4. Curiosity Builds Empathy Because It's a Conduit for Connection
5. Questioning Incongruence Curiously Not Only Builds Empathy, It Enhances Innovation
6. Innovative Ideas are Generated When We are Curious About Human Imperfection and Incongruency
7. Curiosity Builds Compassion for Self and Empathy for Others

FIRESTARTER FUEL—IGNITING ME

1. What are you sure about in your own beliefs?
2. What do others around you think they know about you that does not feel true?
3. What does the "gentle" voice inside you say when you question your own beliefs?
4. What can you observe within yourself with curiosity instead of judgment? This sentence stem can help: "I wonder why I _____ when _____."

FIRESTARTER FUEL—IGNITING WE

1. Who in your life (personal or work) do you not understand or judge often?
2. What would happen if you put on the hat of curiosity and observed them with that lens?

3. When curious, what question would you ask them to satisfy your curiosity? What do you wonder?
4. In what way could you use curiosity to help you solve a challenge in your life currently?

CHAPTER 14

PLAY

I had no choice—it was time to stop for gas. I exited off the long, flat highway connecting Dallas to Lubbock with hesitation because these dry, desolate, windblown towns dotting the path as we drove west were few and far between.

I was with my eighteen-month-old daughter, and knew she would likely need a diaper change, too. The gas stations were dirty, filled with grime due to years of neglect. I was a little creeped out with the idea of my baby and I stopping in this forlorn gas station by ourselves. But the fact remained, we were almost out of gas. The alternative was running out of gas, which frightened me more.

"How are you doing, sweetie?" I smiled, catching her eye in the rearview mirror.

She smiled warmly back, looking up for a second from her iPad. She was watching her favorite Doc McStuffins video. "Okay mommy," she said and went back to the Doc.

She was bright-eyed and full of vigor, curiosity, and determination.

I was ready to get there. We were four hours into the drive.

Trying to change a toddler's diaper in a dirty bathroom was not ideal. It would take a lot of maneuvering.

"Mommy, I do it myself," she said as I tried to pull her out of the car seat to carry her on my hip. I breathed heavily with impatience.

"Okay," I said to her proudly, feeling desperate to get in and out of this situation quickly yet wanting to allow her independence. I touched her diaper as she climbed down from the car, *Good, it was only wet*, I thought.

I continued the planning in my head. *I'll give the attendant my card. Get her into the bathroom, let her stand while I quickly change the diaper. In and out. Easy.*

Inside the station store was worse than I expected—exceptionally rundown.

As I walked into the one-stall, gender-neutral bathroom, I gasped for air. The dirt, grime, and other unwanted debris on the bathroom floor had not only created stains along the lower walls but yellowing also crept from the outer edges of the floor toward the middle. The smell was nauseating.

I looked over at the toilet, deciding I could wait. A slow drip from behind it created wetness around the bottom. The sink, from years of use, looked dirtier than the toilet. I willed myself to hold my own need to go. I held her hand tighter as I used the bottom end of my shirt to lock the door.

She, unlike me, was excited about the adventure. She smiled with the brightest eyes as I repeated for the fourth time, "Do not touch anything. No matter what you do, don't touch anything. It is very dirty in here and we want to leave here cleaner than we came."

WHEN WE PLAY, OUR BRAINS FIND A WAY
I remember noticing a filthy round barrel trashcan directly in front of the toilet, just out of arm's reach.

As I put the diaper bag on the floor, I noted to myself to sanitize the bottom of it as soon as we were back in the car.

"I'm going to change your diaper, but I have to do it with you standing up, not laying down because there's really nowhere for you to lay here." I looked down again horrified at this situation but said to her. "Then, we're going to wash our hands and leave, okay?"

She nodded, still excited for this new adventure. She earnestly complied. As I took her diaper off, I realized too late I had been incorrect—it was not just a wet diaper. It was a dirty, very dirty, one. And for the first time in eighteen months, I was nauseated changing one of her diapers. It was system overload of my senses.

I began hurriedly trying to find the necessary tools to clean up the mess. Her diaper was now halfway off, and with both head and hands focused on the contents of the diaper bag, I frantically searched for a fresh one and wipes. Without looking, I continued to talk to her in the calmest voice I could muster. "Honey, please be still. I just need to wipe you down, sweetie."

"Shit," I whispered to myself. Literally and figuratively.

I worked relentlessly, until I was proud that I had her as clean as possible, I reached around her protruding belly to stick the side tabs of the diaper on. I finally glanced up from my focus on something besides her dirty bottom. And that's when I saw it.

In the middle of my sentence of affirming, encouraging words, "Great work standing so still…" I stopped, and then shrieked.

"Oh my God, what are you doing?" I gasped instinctively. Although I had noticed she was bent over, making it easy for me to clean her bottom, what I did not notice was she was holding herself up using only *her tongue* on the edge of the dirty filthy barrel trash can for support.

Her hands spread were spread widely from her little body on each side the whole time so she was "not touching" as instructed. At least with her fingers. She had been waiting patiently using her tongue for trashcan support.

She glanced, smiling as she continued to hold her tongue, directly licking the trashcan's edge. Kept it there, grinning bigger with eyes shining. In my horror, I hastily yanked her whole body away so that she finally released her tongue from the disgusting, chipping metal garbage can.

In my desperation, I leaned her over the sink, asking her to spit before she swallowed. I looked around for what else could help the damage. *How do you sanitize a tongue?* I thought. She looked at me confused as I showed her how to spit into the sink.

Finally, dejected knowing the damage was done, I asked again, a bit more calmly, "Honey what in the world were you doing? I told you not to touch anything."

Cheerily she said as she held her clean hands up toward mine as if to prove herself, "I didn't!" she claimed proudly.

"But you were touching... with your tongue." I tried to convince her. She shook her head, starting to get tears in her eyes at me denying her reality. She maintained her position, and crossed her arms, pouting now. "No, mommy. I playing."

She was playing.

Thinking back on that day, knowing now that she didn't die or become permanently damaged from the bacteria that day in the dirty bathroom, I can almost hear her little mind whirring away. *Mommy says I can't touch. I wonder... if instead I could do this? Let's see if this will work.*

She found a way to touch the trashcan her way, through play.

PLAY IS IN OUR ORIGINAL BLUEPRINT

We start out with a desire to expand, to learn, through play. We begin this way.

Our nature is to explore, to understand and learn and make sense of our environment—to play with it.

Child psychologists and researchers know the benefits of play in the development of children. In fact, "play therapy" has become a primary approach to therapy because among many other benefits, it helps children:

- express what is troubling them when they do not have verbal language
- develop a foundation for learning
- learn confidence in their ability to solve a problem,
- develop reasoning or executive functioning skills by testing hypothesis
- solve problems using the whole brain—both convergent and divergent problems

My daughter was playing with the dirty trashcan that day trying to learn and make sense of her environment in a creative way. She took the "guardrails" I had given her and found ways to explore given those.

THE PLAYGROUND IS SHRINKING

But over time, our playground shrinks. Our parents teach us what to touch and how to touch it. Over the years, as we are told what to do and not to do, our guardrails narrow to keep us safe.

And in our safety, over time, we forget to play. Instead, we learn how to produce, perform, and perfect.

Melissa Bernstein, co-founder of the toy company, Melissa and Doug, conducted a study in 2018 with Gallup and found that children were spending more time on devices than engaged in either indoor or outdoor free play (Nania, 2018). That trend has continued.

A white paper produced by the *American Journal of Play* in 2011, links the decline of play in the United States culture with the rise of psychopathology in children and adolescents, stating that, "Play, especially social play with other children, serves a variety of developmental functions, all of which promote children's mental health. In the absence of such play, children fail to acquire the social and emotional skills that are essential for healthy psychological development." It goes on to talk about the debilitating effects of this trend, including anxiety, depression, feelings of helplessness, and narcissism, childhood obesity, and ADHD (Gray, 2011).

"Without [play]," said Melissa, "you will never discover who you are and what brings you joy. It is through childhood and play that we discover what we love and what makes us tick."

GAMIFYING WORK CREATES CONNECTION AND INNOVATIVE THINKING

Ironically, I had an upbringing that combined intense work with loads of gamified play.

Starting at about age ten, my summers on the farm were not spent like many children my age. There were no bike rides with neighborhood children or playing in a pool or even lounging around watching TV. They were spent behind the back of a tractor, seated on an implement. An implement is a piece of machinery designed to help do some of the tasks involved in growing a crop such as seeding, cultivating, plowing, or sowing.

In the summers, I sat on an implement we called a "spray rig."

Imagine a fork with the handle attached to the back of a tractor. And the three tines of the fork each with a seat and an umbrella. Each seat was designed to hover over a row of cotton. A large tank of Roundup sat behind the middle seat with three hydraulic lines connecting to our spray guns.

I will never forget the first time my dad hauled us (my sister, age eight, our cousin who visited every summer, age nine, and me) onto the large machinery.

"Okay, everyone take a seat. Your mom is going to drive the tractor. The purpose is for you to use the gun and spray the weeds so they won't overrun the cotton." He showed us how it worked as he talked, spraying some of the bright pink liquid onto the ground.

He went on. "Your job is to stay awake, look for weeds, spray those, and nothing else. This is expensive, so nothing except the weeds. Did you hear me, girls? And no funny business."

These were the days before Roundup hit the news. We did not have hazmat suits. Just three children, waiting for weeds to come upon them as they sat for hours behind a tractor with a mother driving who was almost as bored as we were.

I sat in the hot sun, most of the time under a personal umbrella. Hours, days, weeks, and summers went by slowly in our mission to spray the weeds in the field. We watched row after row of cotton, ready with our hand-held spray guns loaded with Roundup ammunition for the unsuspecting weeds lurking amongst the budding cotton.

Those were our dog days of summer. I have not done the math on the speed of the tractor, the length of the rows, the number of breaks taken, but I can tell you that with the acreage we had and the rows of cotton to cover in 100° plus heat even with an umbrella shade covering most of the day, they were very, very long days.

What I do know is that boredom eventually gives way to imagination if you allow it.

We did not have handheld music devices, let alone iPhones. We only had our minds and each other's companionship and banter. Much of my memory of this intensely mundane existence is ironically, mingled with the fun we had. We managed to reframe this existence to play. We found ways to create because we were constantly innovating to increase the fun and overcome the heat, dust, and boredom. All in all, we:

- learned how to make castles out of tumbleweeds,
- built a zoo of lizards, rabbits, and other scurrying creatures,
- held championship competitions on who could kill the most weeds

Year after year, we created games to move us from the boredom of our work to a spirit of innovation through play. The games we played changed but what did not change was our ability to create through connected play.

PLAY PROMOTES CREATIVE THINKING THROUGH EXPERIMENTATION

I look back on that child I was and hardly recognize her some days. Her ability to play while working was admirable. I have found myself wondering in my most difficult work tasks, *How can I see this as play instead of work?* In my desperation to "figure it out," one day I asked my daughter, "Why do you like to play?"

And she said: "Playing is like my birthday, Mom because when I'm playing and on my birthday, I feel like an adult. The most important part of playing is that I get to make all the rules. That's what we have to do when we play, Mom. We just make up the rules."

To her, play feels like adulting. Ironic that the reality for most adults is that we forget to play, or even how to play.

As a part of writing this book, I had several teachers ask their students what the point of play is, and their answers surrounded this one theme: the joy of experiential learning which promotes the desire to create. Here are some examples of their brilliant thinking.

From one nine-year-old girl: "Children play to find themselves, who they really are—not the mask that the human mass has forced on their face, but who they are underneath. Then they go from there and try new things until they find it. They find what they like, not what others like and they can be free."

And from another ten-year-old boy: "Play is good because you may learn something you did not learn before and it's a form of entertainment for yourself and the person you're playing with. It makes it more fun to be with yourself and others."

As adults, we call that experimentation, which is what innovation produces.

We often believe that productivity should take the place of playing because we're taught that it is part of "adulting." But when we stop playing, we can lose the desire for our natural inclination as humans to grow, experiment, and learn.

PLAYING IS PRODUCTIVE BECAUSE IT PROMOTES PURPOSE AND PASSION.

Ironically, play helps us achieve our goals and to produce in an indirect way. Play promotes producing what matters by giving us the key ingredients for it: purpose and passion.

Our brains activate when we play. Play not only increases our individual productivity, but it also increases desire to work together and collaborate. The point of play is fun, entertainment, and learning something new. It gives us joy and makes us happy. When we experience the emotions of joy and the accomplishment of learning something new, we are more likely to take that learning and produce from it. It fills us with gratitude and a sense of wonder.

In a study by Brigham Young University, teams that played a collaborative video game together for just forty-five minutes were able to increase their productivity on a task by 20 percent (Hollingshead, 2019).

PLAY BUILDS THE EMPATHY
MUSCLE THROUGH PERSPECTIVE TAKING

Studies show that empathy increases with play. One such study on using digital games as "empathy machines," authored by UNESCO's Mahatma Gandhi Institute of Education for Peace and Sustainable Development explored how empathy could be built through gaming. They discovered that when players become immersed in game worlds by taking control (agency) of avatars (digital on-screen representation), it offers unique opportunities for "perspective-taking" (Farber, 2018). Perspective-taking is the ability to look beyond your own point of view so that you can consider how someone else may think or feel about something. It is a form of empathy.

In the same way, a family or group of friends who play Pictionary will draw, act out, or do anything to get their collaborating team members to "understand" them in their effort to "win." This same spirit of play works for any collaborative, innovative endeavor.

When play-based collaboration is enabled, it is easier for a group or team to work together toward a common goal.

Innovation requires play. It requires a sense of wonder, a sense of creating the rules in your mind first, then experimenting with those ideas.

In order to innovate with empathy, we must be willing to learn how to play again, even if it means getting your tongue a little dirty.

FIRESTARTER SPARKS—EMPATHY IS AMPLIFIED WHEN PLAY ACTIVATES PURPOSE AND PASSION

1. When We Play Our Brains Find a Way
2. Play Is in Our Original Blueprint
3. The Playground Is Shrinking
4. Gamifying Work Creates Connection and Innovative Thinking
5. Playing Promotes Creative Thinking through Experimentation
6. Playing is Productive because It Promotes Purpose and Passion
7. Play Builds the Empathy Muscle through Perspective-Taking

FIRESTARTER FUEL—IGNITING ME

1. What type of play do you enjoy most?
2. How can you connect with others through play?
3. What in your life seems the most exhausting? What would make it more fun?

FIRESTARTER FUEL—IGNITING WE

1. Who do you want to connect or collaborate with through play to develop a better working relationship?
2. How can you turn your more mundane work into a game?
3. What could your team reframe into a game of friendly competition?
4. What series of "rewards" could you create to develop playful purpose and passion to lofty goals?

CHAPTER 15

DETACHMENT

The Doberman pressed himself next to me as his mouth curled slightly upward, exposing all his extraordinarily sharp teeth. I looked down to my right where he was starting a very low, almost non-audible growl. If I had not known better, it sounded more like a purr. I noticed my chest was hurting, my heart was beating so fast.

I looked across the aisle of the Southwest plane, past the small girl, to the very intimidating man who was yelling at me. He waved his hands wildly, searching with his left index finger for the attendant call button. We were both sitting in the bulkhead and so was my daughter. We had just boarded a flight and I could sense the anxiety as soon as we boarded. We were at what we thought was the tail end of COVID and nerves were raw. Emotions normally suppressed were at the surface.

"Get your bag off my tennis shoes," the man yelled at me again.

Just a few minutes before we had boarded, with a goal to keep my daughter both physically and emotionally safe, I had leaned down and whispered to her just before the boarding process began, "What do you think would make you feel better—choosing a seat on a row that is empty and wait to see who sits next to us *or* intentionally choosing to sit next to someone who seems kind and safe?"

She looked up, thought for a second then said, "I want to choose who I sit next to."

I smiled and replied, "Me too. I'll follow you and you tell me when you find who it will be."

So, with a smile, I noticed as soon as we boarded that there in the first-row bulkhead, our travel partner would not only include a young Army Veteran with kind eyes but also his enormous Doberman Pincher dog. A red cloth saddle was buckled around the dog's sleek muscular body with a clear label "Emotional Support Dog." My daughter looked up immediately, eyes big, questioning, *What do you think, Mom?* without saying a word.

So, I mirrored her question out loud: "What do you think? Is this who we're sitting next to?"

She nodded profusely and smiled behind her mask. I said, "Do you want to sit in the middle?" Again, a little more reluctantly, she nodded this time her question directed at the young man. She wasn't sure how to move the large dog away from the middle seat so she could sit down. His owner smiled brightly as he gently, but with strength, moved the dog so we could sit.

DETACHING FROM EMOTION HELPS US SEE OBJECTIVELY

And as soon as we sat, the dog laid himself—head, neck, and shoulder—onto my daughter's lap. All six of our hands began simultaneously massaging his beautiful lean muscles as he nuzzled closer and closer taking it in.

We were immediately taken with him and he with us, and his owner gently laughed, saying, "Wow, it looks as if he was waiting for you." The dog, Samuel, then came for me, nuzzling his way onto my lap. We all chuckled at his deep affection for two strangers. I noticed the passengers around us taking it in as well. It was an incredible sight to see this gigantic dangerous-looking dog, nuzzling like a kitten pressing into us. I swear I heard him purring.

So, when I, now in good humor, lifted him up off my lap enough to put mine and my daughter's things in the overhead bin, I said brightly to no one as I noticed tennis shoes taking up the entire bulkhead overhead space, "I see some tennis shoes up here, do you mind if I put my bag here as well?" I looked around to see whose they were, while I politely asked for permission. I knew I would need easy access to the number of things my daughter would inevitably ask for.

And then, directly across from me, I saw the shoes' owner as a man scowled up at me, and said angrily, "Get your bag off of my shoes... now."

That's when I noticed Samuel, the support dog, pressing heavily up against me. His pressure softened and allowed my breath to slow down. It was as if I was in slow motion, as I simultaneously stepped outside of myself observing what was going on while experiencing it. I had been in situations before on flights where this type of emotional anger and reactivity toward me from another passenger would have caused one of following three reactions in me.

Depending on the day, I could have easily reacted—in this order:

1. Fight: "Why don't you move your shoes and put them where they're supposed to be? Don't you know the rule is to allow room overhead for bags?"
2. Flee: "I'm sorry, of course, let me move my bag."
3. Freeze: Say nothing. Blink slowly, become numb and not sure what to do.

Instead, something incredible happened. Calmly, I said, "There's room for both of our things if you don't mind me moving your shoes. But I need to put this bag here so my daughter and I can get our things after we take off."

This made him angrier. He raised his voice louder, and said, not hearing me, "You can put your things back there. I don't care where you put it but move it off my shoes."

With Samuel's presence and pressure increasing as he felt the attack on me, I felt myself breathe again. This time Samuel stepped up in front of me, his ears laid completely down across the back of his head. Still only a purr of a growl, but the snarl increased. His muscles were tense, and I said, calmly, "Let's get someone to help us sort this out."

The flight attendant appeared, and when the man angrily told her I needed to move my bag, she took one look at Samuel and said in full fear: "This is more than I know how to deal with." She promptly went to talk to the captain. I wish I could have heard her whisper. I am assuming it was something like, "I've got a shit show here—a large Doberman is about to attack a man whose shoes are underneath someone else's bag. I'm not sure what to do."

I stayed steady, calm, emotions regulated; I was detached. It was easy for me to stabilize as I felt the support generating from the dog's heat on my thigh.

THROUGH DETACHMENT WE FIND ACCEPTANCE

Promptly, another man from the airline, a ticketing agent, was called to the plane. Clearly, he had been trained in negotiating. "What's wrong, sir?"

The angry man answered, face red, enraged, "Her bag is on my shoes," he seethed, hardly controlling himself.

And then the ticketing agent replied, "You mean this one?"

"Yes," the man said in a growl.

The flight attendant looked at me, turned to act as if he had moved my bag, and said to the man, "It's okay, the bags are not on your shoes, sir. They are just right next to them, okay?"

The man finally exhaled, losing his steam. "Yes, that's fine," he gruffly hem-hawed. And simultaneously Samuel relaxed a bit, falling on me, toward me. This time, I picked his heavy two legs up onto my lap, putting my arms around him.

It took a few seconds as we all recovered to relax but this incredible moment was not lost on anyone who could see and hear the interaction. It was quite magical—to see an attack dog handle an emotionally charged situation, not with his teeth or physical strength, but with his emotional strength of empathy.

There was acceptance in the air finally. The large man accepted my bag would stay close to his big tennies once he detached from his emotion, and I accepted his emotions without trying to fight, flee, or freeze because I was detached with the help of an amazing emotional support dog. Through detachment, I found acceptance in the situation.

DETACHED ACCEPTANCE BUILDS EMPATHY

Acceptance is often misunderstood. It does not mean accepting others' bad behavior without accountability. It does not mean submitting to bullying or people crossing our boundaries. It means accepting something or someone as they are. It means detaching from their view enough to acknowledge it (a situation, person, emotion, etc.) without trying to change it.

When I was supported by a dog that helped me breathe through my own uncomfortable emotions, he helped me detach from the situation and practice the concept of acceptance as a self-regulation strategy.

When we accept, then acknowledge with empathy, without finding judgment or resisting the situation, it allows pure potentiality. It creates space for empathy to step in and let things be. And from a state of just being, opportunity or potential is created. It is the "being with" without trying to change things that allows innovation to unfold.

I left that situation recognizing a powerful truth. I could accept the man's emotional reaction (along with my own) when I could witness the emotions without resisting them. By detaching from his anger and accepting what it was, it allowed us to move through the moment without a complete eruption.

But to do that, I had some emotional support from a dog who helped me detach from my own feelings about the situation. Often when we are caught up in an emotional situation, it's hard to detach. But choosing to detach is the gateway to building acceptance and ultimately, empathy.

DETACHMENT AS THE GATEWAY TO CREATION

I was reminded of the importance of detachment when working on a project—the third I had conducted with this team regarding the subject of brushing teeth. The team wanted to find a way to emotionally connect with consumers about a new toothbrush. If you have been on the toothbrush aisle of any store, you will know there are lots of choices, which makes innovation more challenging. For categories like this, we call this a "crowded space."

So, the team was frustrated. The two times we had conducted research, we had netted with the team wanting to communicate about "tartar control" even though we knew this was not an emotionally resonating space at the time for consumers. But the team was stuck—product developers wanted to stay true to what they could deliver and marketing wanted to create an emotional resonance to draw consumers to purchase.

And no one wanted to listen to the insights. Several new findings had been uncovered in our research, things like how consumers wanted their breath to smell when kissing or cuddling with a loved one. Those are what I call "white space" opportunities and the root of where we could go to approach the problem.

The marketing leader emphatically would say, "We all know tartar control is a cost of entry! We can't talk about that. It has to be more emotionally sexy than that!"

And the product development lead would respond just as enthusiastically, "We can't promise they will get better kisses just because they want that!"

In some ways, they were both "right" to some extent, but their problem was they had stopped listening and both were simultaneously adamant about their separate positions. Then something incredible happened. The door opened and several "suits" walked in. Evidently, while we were at research, a merger had been announced and just like that, the two leaders arguing were walked out and two fresh leaders were walked in—one marketing and one product developer. The "suits" introduced them then left as well. One suit, on his way out, had looked back before shutting the door and said, "I thought it would be good to let our new team members learn as they get geared up for their new roles."

And just like that, we were all faced with a new set of team dynamics and a big problem still to solve. Yet, they were both eager to learn.

The rest of us who were not escorted out looked a little baffled. I was the only one there who did not work for the company. Gathering my wits, I said, "Okay, here's the thing. We have an hour. Our goal is to brief you on what we know and as you are listening, I would love to know what questions you have. The more I understand what you need to know, the easier it is to get you the answers."

The rest of that project was phenomenal. Detached from their own points of view (because they did not yet have one) and eager to learn what they did not know, they soaked up everything. And guess what? The team collaborated and a completely new white space was created—one that helped consumers link the idea of tartar control with giving and receiving better kisses. They logically worked their way into a product development solution that also emotionally resonated with consumers.

That is detachment in its purest form. By removing their own emotional attachment to what was produced, potential was created in the "liminal space."

Later one of the other team members who had been there through all three of the projects said, "You know, at first when I saw both our marketing and product development leader being walked out, I felt bad for them. I had a lot of sympathy for their situation. But after being here with a fresh perspective, and knowing they will land on their feet, I realize that sympathy or feeling sorry for them, does not really help them or me. When I accepted there was a change in leadership and allowed myself to just be with it, things started getting fun. In fact, I'm excited for what we're about to create."

ATTACHED SYMPATHY STIFLES, DETACHED EMPATHY ENABLES

Often the terms sympathy and empathy are used interchangeably but they are not the same. They are quite different. Sympathy occurs when we attach to other people's challenges, frustrations, and desires. So, our go-to response from a sympathetic lens may be to want to fix or help or solve a problem.

When we are attached, we can get into a mental thinking loop to "help" that person which can show up as controlling and thus can cause disconnection instead of connection. Here's how:

1. Attachment increases desire to help
2. Desire to help fuels "solution questioning"
3. "Solution questioning" activates linear thinking
4. Linear thinking leads to emotional stagnation
5. Emotional stagnation leads to lack of connection, apathy, and possibility

But with empathetic detachment, creative thinking arises based on acceptance or "being with" someone and their emotions. Here is how:

1. Detachment increases curiosity
2. Curiosity fuels empathetic questioning
3. Empathetic questioning creates greater understanding
4. Greater understanding activates heart-minded thinking
5. Heart-minded thinking leads to inspiration
6. Inspiration leads to creativity

So, the upward spiral of empathy through acceptance and detachment brings about the connection, creativity, and eventual heart-minded solutions we desire.

FIRESTARTER SPARKS—EMPATHY IS AMPLIFIED THROUGH DETACHED ACCEPTANCE

1. Detaching from Emotion Helps Us See Objectively
2. Through Detachment We Find Acceptance
3. Detached Acceptance Builds Empathy
4. Detachment as the Gateway to Creation
5. Attached Sympathy Stifles, Detached Empathy Enables

FIRESTARTER FUEL—IGNITING ME:

1. What outcome do you think about often and are attached to?
2. Could you welcome another outcome? What if _____ were to happen instead? Then what?
3. What if you did not care about this outcome, what would you choose to do?

FIRESTARTER FUEL—IGNITING WE

1. What do we believe the team should do?
2. Why are we attached to that belief?
3. Could we welcome the team going in a different direction? What if _____ were to happen instead? Then what?
4. What if we did not care about the outcome we see as best, what else could we do?

CHAPTER 16

PRESENCE

The horses' hooves plodded along the worn, dusty, dirt road behind my parents' house, putting distance between us and them. Clickety-click-click-click. Clickety-click-click-click. I still remember the slow, rhythmic, methodical sound and feel of the horse underneath me in the dry West Texas heat. As we moved together, me sitting atop this large, black beautiful beast, my horse, Jake, I felt the freedom I yearned for.

These were my favorite moments in those days. I was thirteen, a bright-eyed early teen with curly, disheveled bright red hair. Life was maddening at that age. I was swarming with thoughts about my parents who I thought were "demanding and controlling." And friends that were on their best days "great" and others "utterly confusing."

But here, on this narrow, dusty dirt road, hidden amongst rows and rows of cotton plants, Jake walked me slowly away from the chaos of my life, giving me the opportunity to feel again. Our bodies moved together in an odd sort of dance. Each step he took created a gentle rocking.

The longer we rode, the calmer I became. The arguing voices were distant now and in the past.

It was mid-August, and my mouth was parched. The wind picked up a bit, swirling the unsettled dust into a little mini West-Texas tornado just in front of us, then drifted off disappearing into more dryness.

Jake's ears flickered. He sensed a scurrying animal in the distance before I did, helping me turn my attention back to the present surroundings. Here we were, the two of us, free.

In late summers at dusk, the hot dry dust would turn the sky into the most brilliant sunsets. Our back was to it this evening, and I could begin to see our shadows on the ground leading us forward.

Slowly, as the distance grew between us and my home, my awareness of the present surroundings increased. And, as if on cue, Jake stopped and turned his head back toward me, as if to say, *Look. Here. Now. See what I have to show you?* He whinnied.

PRESENCE ALLOWS US TO DISCOVER WHAT IS HIDDEN ON THE SURFACE

At some point in the ride he began to lead, probably because my mind was so preoccupied as I recollected the heated "debate" between my mom and me that I forgot where I was. And then I saw it, the most amazing sight

I had ever witnessed on the West Texas Plains. I giggled to myself as I sat in shock at the show I was suddenly audience to.

It struck me as odd, so close to the home where I had decided nothing was new or interesting. I was so accustomed to seeing the same long, brown rows of dirt. Depending on the season, sometimes white pockets of cotton added to the view. But never this.

Before my very eyes, I was witnessing a small army of prairie dogs sitting, front legs poised sweetly and daintily on their chest for as far as I could see across the flat, barren pasture they were nestled on and around the small mounds beneath them. What I know now was that underneath the ground between their mounds, a labyrinth of complex, beautiful community lay underneath. Prairie dogs are what scientists call a "keystone species" or "ecosystem engineer," which means their species helps define and maintain the health and stability of an entire ecosystem (Boyce, 2020).

Prairie dogs create separate housing for their toilets, food, and individual family units. We had just approached a lively community of them, and they were wondering about us—curious and attuned. As I heard one of their cute dog barks, and then another replied with a slightly different bark, like two actual dogs—a poodle and St. Bernard. I giggled again at their barks and was in awe at the sheer number of these small, cute creatures looking at me as we discovered each other for the first time.

After about three minutes of our staring game with mutual wonder and delight, our frozen space of dual connection was broken. Perhaps their leader gave them the green light on Jake and me. They stopped their staring and began moving, getting busy going about their day.

Starting that day, and for weeks to come, Jake and I made our way from the bustling farm to experience our private little community. We were fascinated with our secret discovery.

PRESENCE CREATES SAFETY, SAFETY CREATES DEEPER CONNECTION

They were evidently fascinated by us and wanted to show off their skills. Over time, as they grew more comfortable with our presence, the more we experienced their magical movie.

In fact, what I learned due to our consistent, quiet presence with them was their barking sounds shifted and changed along with their body movements. They would scurry together in a group, and soon we noticed that some would kiss.

They approached each other, embraced in a hug while they locked their faces (teeth) together. Now I know this kissing pattern helps their survival. By locking teeth, they recognize their allies versus enemies (Gammon, 2014). While I did not understand any of this at the time, I would laugh out loud each time I saw them locked together in a deep kiss.

By simply being there, present, they seemed to enjoy sharing their life with us. They were comfortable just being prairie dogs. After about a week of our visits, they would begin their barking as we approached them. As it turns out, prairie dogs have one of the most complex communication and social systems of any animal, according to scientist Con Slobodchikoff at Northern Arizona State University in Flagstaff, Arizona (Crew, 2014). While I did not possess the language for what they were trying to tell us, we were deeply connected

Through presence, Jake and I bore witness to a unique wonder of the world. This animal species gave us the gift of experiencing something very few people get to see. And in the middle of a dusty farm on the plains of West Texas, I became more connected to myself, my home, and a larger community than I ever knew existed.

It was way better than watching TV. The entertainment of each of our private prairie dog moments was one of the delights of my adolescence.

PRESENCE HELPS CREATE A SENSE OF PEACE

And through that, I learned that tuning my awareness to the present can bring immense joy and miraculous peace as new possibilities rise to the surface.

That's the power of presence: peace. The power of being in the present moment, with mind fully attuned to what is directly in front of you gives something that the past or the future cannot. It gives us the possibility of loving what is. And loving what is right in front of you creates space for more love to come in.

Byron Katie in her acclaimed book, *Loving What Is: Four Questions That Can Change Your Life*, says, "Peace doesn't require two people; it requires only one. It has to be you. The problem begins and ends there."

She goes on to say, "I am a lover of what is, not because I'm a spiritual person, but because it hurts when I argue with reality."

Shauna Niequist says it well in her book, *Present over Perfect: Leaving Behind Frantic for a Simpler, More Soulful Way of Living*: "I used to believe, in the deepest way, that there was something irreparably wrong with me. And love was a lie. Now I'm beginning to see that love is the truth and the darkness is a lie."

She goes on to say, "It's in the silence that you can finally allow yourself to be seen, and it's in the being seen that healing and groundedness can begin."

Presence silences us, and in the silence we become an observer of what is actually there. When we are present, we can be with ourself and others without fear, worry, sadness, or anger filtering our view. We simply allow whatever is going on to be what it is. And with the allowing, our ability to see things and people (and ourselves) for what they are increases. We amplify our ability to empathize.

Presence pulls us out of our "monkey mind" which is constantly overworking.

PRESENCE GETS HIJACKED WITH THE MONKEY MIND

What stops us from being present is our wandering mind typically, attempting to "pre-solve" what will happen in the future or "wanting to fix" what has happened in the past.

These two states of being are what many scientists and others call the "monkey mind."

The story of the monkey mind is rooted in an interesting story according to Tiffany Erickson in her blog post "Let Go of The Bananas:" "way down on the South Sea island of Borneo, where the natives go about catching monkeys in a very unusual way.

Most of the monkeys are sold to zoos, so the hunters avoid using ordinary traps which can cause disfiguring injuries. Instead, they hollow out a football-sized coconut, leaving a hole in one end just big enough for a monkey to slip in its hand. Inside the hollowed-out coconut, the natives put delicious green bananas, the monkey's favorite food. They screw a strong eyebolt into the solid end of the coconut. Then they fasten a chain to the eyebolt and tie the other end of the chain to the roots of a nearby tree. The trap—for it is a trap—is almost ready. Just before they leave, the natives scatter more green bananas around the jungle clearing.

Then they return to their villages.

When a troop of monkeys comes swinging through the rain forest, the sharpest-eyed among them will usually see the green bananas in the clearing. That monkey will signal the troop to halt, and they'll descend, jabbering and chattering, to scoop up their favorite food. When all of the freebies are gone, one of them will pick up the baited coconut, put their hand through the hole in one end, and clutch the bananas inside with their fist. However, when they try to pull out the delicious fruit, they quickly discover that the hole in the coconut is too small for them to withdraw the banana-filled hand. All the monkey has to do to escape is open their fist and let go of the bananas. Then they can easily pull out their hand.

Alas, the greedy monkey almost never does the logical thing. They try to carry off the coconut, but of course, it's chained securely to a tree. They struggle, they scream, they rage, they foam, they tug and pull at the coconut until their wrist is raw and bleeding, and they themself are exhausted. When the natives come back next morning to check their trap, they find a battered, broken-spirited monkey who's been caught by its own fist" (Erickson, 2016).

The Monkey was so caught up in the thought of enjoying the banana in the future, that he failed to recognize the trap.

I can see this in my own pushing and pulling. I see this every time I am not living in the present.

Presence seems as if it is an easy concept in theory—*just be present* you could tell yourself. But it is often challenging to be fully present because we try to approach presence as a state of doing, instead of being. We are so accustomed to doing that that we simply want an instruction manual for "how" to do it.

"Tell me how to be present," we ask, "and I'll do it." Doing helps us achieve. But being present helps us become attuned to what is happening right now in the moment.

RHYTHM AND ATTUNEMENT HELP US CREATE PRESENCE

So, how do you stop the monkey mind from chattering? That's the trick. Many talk about mindfulness as a way to shift from anxious or sad thoughts.

What I have found from most of my clients, the thousands of people I've interviewed over the years, and with myself, is that once we go into the spiral of the monkey mind, it can be tough to shift out of it.

One of my dear clients said to me one day, "I can try to be mindful, but as much as I want to, once I start down the path of trying to figure something out, my mind won't stop until I have. It literally won't stop."

But what happened that day on the back of my horse, Jake, was something that triggered the shift in my brain from the worry that plagued me to a calmer state of mind as we walked away from the house.

That something was rhythmic riding. As I sat on his back, what I now know I experienced physically was my brain being regulated with a term scientists call "bottom-up regulation" through rhythmic riding (Firing & Wiring). When our brains get triggered by external factors, it creates an arrhythmic pattern, causing our neurons to "overfire" in our amygdala where "fight, flight or freeze" occurs. When something or someone creates "rhythm" for us (a parent rocking a baby), this "bottom area" of our brain, the amygdala (or brain stem) can regulate again. Once regulated, the over-firing of neurons can then work their way up, and into our neocortex getting us back to our executive functioning skills where creativity, connection, and problem-solving can occur (Brickel, 2019).

The rhythm of riding on Jake was enhanced with his attunement to me, helping my neurons stop firing in my lower brainstem (where fight or flight was helping me figure out how to survive my future as a teen). Instead, I could access peace and connectedness.

Attunement is the sensing of others, knowing their rhythm and being with them, connected while allowing them to experience themselves fully (Erksine, 1998). That's what Jake did that day and every day I rode him.

Whether it is rocking, listening to music, or creating a sense of rhythm for the body, often it is this physical movement that can move us back into a state of calm, clarity, and presence. With that, we can connect to what is happening in front of us, present with what is.

Now, I can create this rhythm in my own body, especially when my full presence and empathy is needed. Just standing, rocking back and forth from one foot to another is a simple way to move and shift out of the past or future and back to the present. I notice I do it most in my stressful research projects or when I am on stage. Just simply rocking back and forth or sometimes tapping on both of my knees can help silence my mind, bringing me back to presence, back to observation, back to peace, and back to creating.

FIRESTARTER SPARKS—EMPATHY IS AMPLIFIED AS PRESENCE QUIETS OUR MIND

1. Presence Allows Us to Discover What is Hidden On the Surface
2. Presence Creates Safety, Safety Creates Deeper Connection
3. Presence Builds Empathy through a Sense of Peace
4. Presence Gets Hijacked with the Monkey Mind
5. Rhythm and Attunement Help Us Create Presence

FIRESTARTER FUEL—IGNITING ME:

1. Who are you listening to when I'm having a conversation?
2. What three things would you like to learn from someone when you are in conversation with him or her?
3. What can you focus on in your environment right here, right now?

FIRESTARTER FUEL—IGNITING WE:

1. What person in our team has the least to say? What could we learn from him/her?
2. What question could we ask our team to start our meetings to help us ground in the here and now?
3. How can we be with someone on our team who is struggling with a personal situation to show we are present to their circumstance?

CONCLUSION

THE GIFTS OF INNOVATING WITH EMPATHY

So, what have we learned?

We've learned that although innovation seems like a vast unknown, there's a proven process that helps The Innovator rise up through the unknown by using empathy to problem solve with confidence. While it is non-linear, there are five steps to navigating innovation successfully. The Innovator's Journey is to: uncover desire with heart-led clarity, discover to expand knowledge by listening to learn from the heart, discern by connecting dots to see emotional patterns for design inspiration, design by creating passion-led possibilities, and decide to determine wise direction from holistic understanding.

We've learned there are common emotional barriers to innovation and empathy can bring us back to connected and creating when we find ourselves stuck and disempowered. We can use empathy to transform resistance to acceptance, perfectionism to connection, confusion to confidence, loneliness to gratitude, rigidity to mental agility, overwhelm to faith-filled action.

Above all, we've learned that empathy is a muscle that can be strengthened with four key qualities. Like any muscle, there are ways to build it, including curiosity which builds a bridge, play which activates purpose and passion, detachment which allows acceptance, and presence which quiets our mind. These qualities help us slow down, listen, and be with ourselves and others in a more connected way.

To get there, we've discussed examples from corporate giants who have used empathy to lift the mask in search of deeper human truths and of more powerful innovation. I've used personal stories supplemented with neuroscience, psychology, media studies, and more to bring the power of empathy for innovation to life.

EMPATHY AS A FIRESTARTER

For those of you still wondering about my baby brother who first gave me the metaphor of the importance of using the right FireStarter, he still teaches me about fire—as a fireman. His heroic efforts for the past twenty years helping his community by fighting fires for a living is an example of how any pain can be reframed into a gift. Our pain is not permanent; it can move through us if we allow it.

WHY I WROTE THIS BOOK

Like many of you, I am a seeker, hungry for knowledge. And I spent most of my adulthood seeking the truth of others to build my knowledge bank. And I spent many years with the benefit of seeing the most powerful organizations bring products to life en masse where I could learn to harness the power of emotion through empathy to create amazing things.

I wrote this book because I now know that more important than knowledge is to live with grit, gratitude, grace, and the gifts that come from returning to empathy to solve even the biggest problems. And I wrote it because I know the way to living like that is to create from the heart. And that empathy gives us access to the heart.

If you can remember even one idea in this book and use it to solve a messy problem, create something meaningful, shift an organization to be kinder, or just feel more at peace daily, you'll be helping me with my goal.

In a way, this is a small desire compared to what I'm hoping some of you reading this might create. I'm not trying to solve hunger or water shortage. But I hope by reading this, you will be inspired to step into your life a little braver each day, empowered with momentum toward what you desire for your life.

WHERE TO LOOK FOR MORE ANSWERS

While some of my clients call me "The Empathy Queen," I certainly don't have all the answers on empathy. But

I, like you, am on a constant journey of discovery. I'm passionate about using empathy for innovation because I know it works. I'm learning that like many things that are part magical, part earthly, we don't always understand exactly why or how it works, we just know it does. That's how I feel about empathy in innovation, mainly because I have amazing clients who allow me to learn from their brilliance.

As I continue to integrate all I'm learning about I intend to build a community for future learning.

If you're interested in being a part of a community committed to make more things with empathy, you can visit us at madewithempathy.com and let us know.

And for the seekers who just want the secret ingredient for innovating with empathy, here's the latest one I've found: There's nothing to fix. We are all already enough.

Hopefully this book helps you step into the unknown with that truth.

ACKNOWLEDGEMENTS

If you read to the end of this book and are still reading, I acknowledge you. It's been quite a journey writing this book. It almost didn't happen... many times. My biggest accomplishment was overcoming each and every one of the barriers in Part II and coming back to a place of stillness and presence long enough to turn the fragmented thoughts in my head onto a laptop. Doing so meant learning how to give myself the empathy I wanted to write about—so ironic. To all of my friends and family who encouraged my writing process, edited my words, and put structure to my dreams: I am forever grateful.

To Autumn, my darling daughter, thank you for the constant inspiration and for all you teach me. Your beauty, grace, and love is a salve for my soul. There would be no book without you. And in my heart will always be the chocolate and pumpkin pies you made for me in honor of hitting my deadlines. Getting to be your mom is the biggest treat!

To my "Soul Sisters" Kara Murphy, Susan Capps, Donna Heidkamp, Jessica Serrano, Carrie Cayse, and Jeanne

Lucke who signed up blindly for my online course with patience and grace, and helped me see myself. I am so grateful to call you true friends. You helped me dare.

To my amazing parents Gary and Cynthia Bell. Thank you for raising me to be resilient and for pouring into us your example of the fruits of the spirit.

To my team, Shelley Miller and Lisa Martens who somehow kept the ship afloat while multi-tasking motherhood through the pandemic while keeping me sane and our clients happy through this journey. Thank you!

To my Beta Readers, Carrie Cayse, Chris Hauck, Don Harton, Carli Rosencranz, Donna Heidkamp, Susan Capps. I had a lot of nerve asking you (busy organizational leaders and business owners) to read my whole book and give comments—and during a pandemic, no less! But I'm so grateful for you saying yes and honoring your commitment. This book is so much better because of you.

Big thanks to the entire team at New Degree Press who supported me on my publishing journey. David Grandouiller, Vivian Rose, and Christy Mossburg, you are amazing editors. Thank you especially to Eric Koester of the Creator Institute and Georgetown University for texting me to ask if I "was still interested in joining the program" on the last day to enroll.

Thank you to everyone who participated in my "empathy interviews." These propelled me forward, helped me see light in the tunnel of COVID-19, and grow my empathy as I listened to your experiences, which were all uniquely different than my own.

Thank you to my wonderful clients whose stories I wove together for the purpose of confidentiality. You have been a gift to me in so many ways, and I look forward to more journeying with you. Your strength, resilience, brilliance, and everyday bravery to make better things together are worthy, even on the days it doesn't seem like it.

Thank you to Jesse Antin and the team at Greater Good Science at Berkley. Your research and writing continues to be an inspiration throughout the world. Thank you for the hope you instill.

This book was made possible also by a community of people who believed in me so fervently they preordered their copies and helped promote the book before it even went to print. Thanks to you all for making *The Fire Starter*'s publishing possible:

Alicia Mosley, Amy Guiter, Amy Marie Bella, Shelley Miller, Angela Wood, Angelina Pinto, Angie Littlefield, Barbara Richter, Brenda Busch, Bryan Elder, Carli Rosencranz, Caroline Volpe, Caroline Wilson, Carrie Cayse, Caryn Goldsmith, Casey Bernard, Cathy Sawyer, Chris Walters, Chris Hauck, Christie Pollet Young, Christy Fowler, Christy Hennigan, Claudia Ball, Clint Tillison, Corey Gilbert, Cyndi Bishop, Cynthia Bell, Dana Turner, David Toothaker, Dawn Taylor, Denise Sinisi, Don Harton, DonJay Rice, Donna Heidkamp, Elizabeth Castro, Elvira Sakmari, Eric Koester, Gail Blair, Garry Jones,

Gary Murtha, Gilbert Martinez, Gina Beville, Gretchen Darby, Haley Stomp, Heather Warnke, James Daley, Janiece Ferrell, Jeeti Kahlon, Jeff Schiefelbein, Jessica Serrano, Jill Lynch, Jill Young, John Steelhammer, Kara Murphy, Kari Coursey, Katelyn Salzman, Kathrin Petty, Kathy Presbaugh, Kathy Lyda, Katie Garry, Katja Cahoon, Kelly Bell, Kelly Kitchens, Kelly Smith, Kristen Evan, Krystyna Tengler, Laura Davis, Lauren Kearns, Lauren White, Leah Stone, Lesli Rogers, Lisa Hazen, Lisa Martens, Lourdes Molina, Mai Tolentino, Marie Facini, Marisol Alviso, Marta Villanueva, Patrick Rooney, Matt Lohr, Michael Saunders, Michelle Boggs, Mike Courtney, Muriel M Jernigan, Natalie Orme, Nicole Martinez, Nina Cornwell, Pam Goldfarb Liss, Patricia Mejia, Penny King, Perry Crafton, Ronda Porter, Sandra McKinley, Sarah Horsley, Scott Conlin, ScottGottlich, Scott Holstine, Sharon Pierce, Steve Lown, Susan Capps, Susan Kelly, Suzanne Townley, T Craig Carlton, Tanya Pinto, Tara Ackerman, Tracey & George Kansas, Willis Cantey

APPENDIX:

INTRODUCTION:
Bar Am, Jordan, Laura Fursthenthal, Felicitas Jorge, & Erik Roth. "Innovation in a crisis: Why it is more critical than ever." McKinsey & Company. June 17, 2020. https://www.mckinsey.com/business-functions/strategy-and-corporate-finance/our-insights/innovation-in-a-crisis-why-it-is-more-critical-than-ever

Greater Good Science Center. "What is Empathy?" *Greater Good Magazine*, Accessed June 27, 2021. https://greatergood.berkeley.edu/topic/empathy/definition

IDEO. "Hello I'm David Kelley." Accessed July 19, 2021. https://www.ideo.com/people/david-kelley

CHAPTER 2:
Brown, Brené. "Brené on Day 2." September 20, 2020. In *Unlocking Us*. Produced by Cadence 13. Podcast, 3:00-29:00. https://brenebrown.com/podcast/brene-on-day-2/.

Campbell, Joseph. *The Hero's Journey.* Novato, CA: New World Library, 2014.

Jack AI, Boyatzis RE, Khawaja MS, Passarelli AM, Leckie RL. "Visioning in the brain: an fMRI study of inspirational coaching and mentoring." *Soc Neurosci* 8(4), (2013): 369-84. https://pubmed.ncbi.nlm.nih.gov/23802125/.

McLaren, Karla, *The Art of Empathy: A Complete Guide to Life's Most Essential Skill.* Boulder, CO: Sounds True, Inc, 2013.

Pixar, Ed. *Creativity: Overcoming the Unseen Forces That Stand in the Way of True Inspiration.* New York: Random House, 2014.

CHAPTER 3:

The University of Texas at Austin. "Working Together is Easier if You Can Distinguish Perspective-Taking from Empathy." Last Modified January 9, 2019. https://research.utexas.edu/showcase/articles/view/working-together-is-easier-if-you-can-distinguish-perspective-taking-from-empathy.

CHAPTER 4:

Abha, Marathe & Archana Sen. "Empathetic Reflection: Reflecting with Emotion." *Reflective Practice,* 22:4 (2021) 566–574. https://doi.org/10.1080/14623943.2021.1927693.

Burgos-Robles, Anthony, Katalin M. Gothard, Marie H. Monfils, Alexei Morozov, Aleksandra Vicentic. "Conserved features of anterior cingulate networks support observational learning across species" *Neuroscience & Biobehavioral Reviews,* Volume 107 (2019) Pages 215–228. https://doi.org/10.1016/j.neu-biorev.2019.09.009.

Salem, Richard. "Empathetic Listening" (blog). Accessed on July 6, 2021. http://cultureofempathy.com/Projects/Empa-thy-Movement/References/Reflective-Listening.htm.

CHAPTER 5:

Sims, Peter. "The No. 1 Enemy of Creativity: Fear of Failure." *Harvard Business Review* (blog). December 27, 2017. https://hbr.org/2012/10/the-no-1-enemy-of-creativity-f

Sutherland, Rory. *Alchemy: The Dark Art and Curious Science of Creating Magic.* New York, NY: Harper Collins, 2019.

Tsaousides, Theo Ph.D. "Why Fear of Failure Can Keep You Stuck." *Psychology Today* (blog). October 5, 2012. https://www.psychologytoday.com/us/blog/smashing-the-brain-blocks/201712/why-fear-failure-can-keep-you-stuck

CHAPTER 6:

2E Twice Exceptional Newsletter. "A definition of Twice-Ex-ceptional. August 10, 2021. https://www.2enewsletter.com/topic_2e_aDefinitionOfTwice-exceptionality.html.

Kashtan, Miki. "Flow, Decision-Making, and Conflict." *The Fear-less Heart* (blog). June 11, 2021. https://thefearlessheart.org/flow-decision-making-and-conflict/.

CHAPTER 8:

Kohner, Scott. "The Ugly Side of Perfectionism and Rumination" (blog). Accessed on September 5, 2021. https://scottkohner.com/blog/2018/03/19/the-ugly-side-of-perfectionism-and-rumination/.

Korb, Alex. *Upward Spiral: Using Neuroscience to Reverse the Course of Depression, One small Change at a Time*. Oakland, CA. New Harbinger Publication, 2015.

Smith, Martin M., Simon B. Sherry, Vanja Vidovic, Paul L. Hewitt, and Gordon L. Flett. "Why does perfectionism confer risk for depressive symptoms? A meta-analytic test of the mediating role of stress and social disconnection." *Journal of Research in Personality*, Volume 86, 2020.

CHAPTER 10:

Michelson, Andrea. "People are less lonely when they embrace uncertainty and feel empathy, a study finds." *Insider*, October 1, 2020. https://www.insider.com/people-less-lonely-if-they-have-empathy-compassion-wisdom-study-2020-9.

Simon-Thomas, Emiliana R. "Are the Rich More Lonely? Two new studies disagree about the link between income and social connections." *Greater Good Magazine: WorkPlace Articles & More* (2016). https://greatergood.berkeley.edu/article/item/are_the_rich_more_lonely.

Unger, Rachel "How Loneliness Affects Employee Productivity." *Made of Millions* (blog). Accessed on October 1, 2021.

https://www.madeofmillions.com/articles/how-loneli-ness-affects-employee-productivity.

CHAPTER 11

Doidge, Norman. *The Brain that Changes Itself: Stories of Personal Triumph from the Frontiers of Brain Science.* New York, NY. Viking, 2007.

Exploring your mind. "Blame and Rigid Thinking: They're Undermining Your Mental Health." Accessed May 19, 2021. https://exploringyourmind.com/blame-rigid-thinking-mental-health/.

Koustaal, Wilma. *The Agile Mind.* Oxford, England. Oxford University Press, 2011.

Maisel, Eric. *Brainstorm: Harnessing the Power of Productive Obsessions.* New World Library, 2010.

CHAPTER 12

Hanson, Rick. *Neurodharma: New Science, Ancient Wisdom, and Seven Practices of the Highest Happiness.* New York, NY. Harmony, 2020.

Nagoski, Emily, and Amelia Nagoski. *Burnout: The Secret to Unlocking the Stress Cycle.* New York, NY. Ballantine Books, 2019.

CHAPTER 13

Bryant, Adam. "How to Become a CEO from a Decade's Worth of Them." *New York Times,* October 27, 2017. https://www.nytimes.com/2017/10/27/business/how-to-be-a-ceo.html

Dartmouth Engineering. "Opinions Are Not Facts: How Scientific Curiosity May Save Us." November 4, 2020. https://engineering.dartmouth.edu/news/opinions-are-not-facts-how-scientific-curiosity-may-save-us.

CHAPTER 14

Farber, Matthew. "Teaching Empathy with Video Games." edutopia, April 13, 2018. https://www.edutopia.org/article/teaching-empathy-video-games.

Gray, Peter. "The Decline of Play and the Rise of Psychopathology in Children and Adolescents." *American Journal of Play,* volume 3, number 4, 2011.

Hollingshead, Todd. "Collaborative video games could increase office productivity." BYU News, January 28, 2019. https://news.byu.edu/news/study-collaborative-video-games-could-increase-office-productivity.

Nania, Rachel. "Despite Known Benefits, kids are playing less." *Wtop News,* March 18, 2018. https://wtop.com/parenting/2018/03/study-despite-known-benefits-kids-playing-less/.

CHAPTER 16

Boyce, Andy and Andrew Dreelin. "Ecologists Dig Prairie Dogs, And You Should Too." Smithsonian's National Zoo & Conservation Biology Institute, July 2, 2020. https://nationalzoo.si.edu/conservation-ecology-center/news/ecologists-dig-prairie-dogs-and-you-should-too.

Brickel, Robyn E. "Why a Bottom-Up Approach to Trauma Therapy is So Powerful." Brickel & Associates, LLC, June 4, 2019. https://brickelandassociates.com/bottom-up-approach-to-trauma/.

Crew, Bec. "Catch the Wave: Decoding the Prairie Dog's Contagious Jump-Yips." Scientific American, January 7, 2014. https://blogs.scientificamerican.com/running-ponies/catch-the-wave-decoding-the-prairie-doge28099s-contagious-jump-yips/.

Erickson, Tiffany. "Let Go of The Bananas." Raising Lemons, April 4, 2016. https://www.raisinglemons.com/thinker/monkeys-bananas/.

Erksine, R.G., Attunement and Involvement: Therapeutic Responses to Relational Needs. International Journal of Psychotherapy, Vol. 3 No. 3, 1998, https://counselling-vancouver.com/attunement/.

Firing & Wiring. "Rhythmic Riding." Accessed July 25, 2021. https://mycreswickfellowshiptour.wordpress.com/2014/06/26/rhythmic-riding/.

Gammon, Katherine. "Scientists Unlock the Secret to Prairie Dogs' Social Networks to Save Them." Take Part, August 1, 2014.

http://www.takepart.com/article/2014/07/31/scientists-unlock-secret-prairie-dogs-social-networks-save-them.

Katie, Byron. *Loving What Is: Four Questions That Can Change Your Life.* New York, NY. Three Rivers Press, 2003.

Niequist, Shauna. *Present Over Perfect: Leaving Behind Frantic for a Simpler, More Soulful Way of Living.* Grand Rapids, MI. Zondervan, 2016.